How *to* WIN *at* GARDENING

How *to* WIN *at* GARDENING

RICHARD JACKSON
and
CAROLYN HUTCHINSON

HarperCollins*Publishers*

First published in 1996 by HarperCollins*Publishers*, London

A CIP catalogue record for this book
is available from the British Library

ISBN 0 00 412988 1

Editorial Director: *Polly Powell*
Project Editor: *Carole McGlynn*
Picture Researcher: *Becky Humphreys*
Consultant for *Garden Answers*: *Adrienne Wild*

Designed and produced by Cooling Brown, Hampton, Middlesex

Colour reproduction by Colourscan, Singapore
Printed and bound in Italy by Rotolito Lombarda SpA, Milan

Acknowledgements
The publishers thank the following for their kind permission to
reproduce the photographs in this book:

David Austin Roses Ltd page 101; **Gillian Beckett** pages 27, 38 (top), 63 (top), 65 (top),
73 (top right), 101 (bottom), 109 (top left); **Deni Bown** pages 71, 73 (top left), 74;
Crown copyright Brogdale pages 37 (top), 40 (top); **The Garden Picture Library**
pages 1 (J. Sira), 52 (Clive Nichols), 55 and 57 (bottom) (John Glover),
58 (top) (Bob Challinor); **Bob Gibbons Natural Image** pages 24, 97, 98, 103 (bottom), 105,
108, 109 (top right), 122, 131 (top), 134 (top middle and right), 135, 136, 137, 138, 139;
John Glover Photography pages 8, 22, 42, 43, 44, 45, 96, 100;
Harkness New Roses page 102 (bottom); **Holt Studios** pages 88, 89, 90, 92,
93 (bottom), 94 (bottom right); **Levingtons/Fisons Horticultural Ltd** page 35 (bottom);
Mattocks Roses of Oxford page 102 (top); **Ken Muir** pages 38 (bottom), 39, 40 (bottom), 41;
Photos Horticultural Picture Library pages 6, 26 (bottom), 36, 59 (bottom), 76, 79, 82, 84,
85, 87, 102, 103 (top), 104, 107 (top), 116, 119, 120 (top), 121, 122, 123, 124; **Stapeley
Water Gardens Ltd, Cheshire** pages 133 (bottom), 134 (top left);
Graham Strong, Garden Folio pages 35 (top), 56, 57 (top right), 66, 120 (bottom),
125, 133 (top); **Suttons Group of Companies Ltd, Torquay, Devon** pages 9, 10 (top), 14,
15 (bottom), 37, 50, 58 (bottom), 59 (top right); **Thompson & Morgan Seeds Ltd (UK)**
page 59 (top left); **Valley Green (UK)** page 64.

All other photographs supplied by *Garden Answers* Magazine.

Contents

INTRODUCTION **6**

BEDDING PLANTS **9**

BULBS **17**

CLIMBERS and WALL SHRUBS **23**

CONTAINER GARDENING **29**

FRUIT **37**

GARDEN PLANNING and DESIGN **43**

GROWING FROM SEEDS and CUTTINGS **49**

HANGING BASKETS **53**

HARDY PERENNIALS **61**

HERBS **67**

HOUSEPLANTS **71**

LAWNS **77**

LOW MAINTENANCE **83**

PESTS and DISEASES **89**

ROSES **97**

SHRUBS **105**

SOIL CARE **111**

TREES **117**

VEGETABLES **125**

WATER GARDENING **131**

WEEDS **137**

INDEX **140**

Introduction

This practical and inspiring book arms gardeners with the knowledge to succeed. Practical advice, based on the real experience of the authors and presented in a lively but informative style, gives the new gardener in particular the confidence to have a go, while providing enough inspiration for any jaded enthusiast to try something new. The book covers all aspects of gardening that interest today's gardeners – from growing plants in containers to ideas for low maintenance – without dwelling too long on traditional techniques that have lost favour with busy gardeners. Packed with planting ideas and expert tips, it shows how to achieve results quickly and easily. The authors deal with problem solving in a down to earth manner, so that keeping weeds in order and pests and diseases at bay can be seen as simple routine rather than a difficult chore. With its recommended plant varieties and practical suggestions for making the most of everything, from roses to hanging baskets, this book provides readers with all they need to know to become expert gardeners!

ADRIENNE WILD

EDITOR

Garden Answers magazine

Bedding plants

You just can't beat bedding plants for sheer flower power. Whether planted in mass blocks, like the popular park bedding schemes of old, or used selectively in small groups, they give a wonderful display for months on end.

Most bedding plants are annuals, lasting only one season, but tender perennials like geraniums and fuchsias can live for years if you cosset them a bit indoors during the winter.

There's only one problem; bedding plants can be hard work. To keep them looking at their best, they need regular watering, feeding and dead-heading. But millions of gardeners know that if you can spare the time, it's well worth the effort for such glorious results.

Sturdy, healthy plug-grown plants are great value for money

GROWING SUCCESS

Bedding plants can be grown from **seed**, and it's certainly the cheapest method, but for gardening beginners it's very much simpler to buy them as plants, which are available at various stages of growth.

Seedlings are supplied in small pots or boxes, each densely sown with around 100 plants. These should be carefully separated (pricked out) and transplanted to seed trays or individual pots of good compost, handling them by the leaves and taking care not to damage roots or stems. In seed trays, space the seedlings at 5cm/2in intervals so that they have room to grow on. Give them a

light position on a windowsill or in a frost-free greenhouse, keep them evenly watered, and they should be ready to plant out by mid-May.

Small **plug grown plants** are individually grown in miniature cells of compost and it's very easy to pop them out of the cells, transfer them to individual 9cm/3½in pots and grow them on indoors before planting out. There's minimal root disturbance, and they should romp away. Plugs are are particularly good value and there's an excellent range to choose from.

Seedlings and plugs are available from early spring but once May is under way, you should find a tempting selection of bedding ready to plant out as soon as possible after the last frost in your area (usually towards the end of the month). These more mature plants are sold in **strips**, **boxes** and **pots**.

Of the three, plants in strips are the cheapest, but they're small and will take a while longer to establish after planting, especially as root

---

PLANTING IN THE GARDEN

To get your plants off to a flying start, it's worth improving the soil by adding some organic matter, like mushroom compost, before planting. It's not essential, but if you do fork in 5-7.5cm/2-3in to the surface, it really will give them a boost.

Water the soil if it's a bit dry, and soak the plants for an hour or so before taking them out of their containers.

Space them out (remembering their eventual spread), then dig the planting holes, each of which should be large enough to take the rootball comfortably at the same level as it was in the pot or strip. Fill in around the rootball, gently firming the soil down. Finally, water the plants in, and keep regularly watered until they have put out new roots and are growing well.

Surfinia petunias are astonishingly vigorous and free-flowering all summer long

Like most plants, bedding plants hate to be waterlogged, so check that your pot has drainage holes, then add a layer of stones, broken pots or lumps of polystyrene to increase the drainage, followed by some potting compost. Bedding plants aren't fussy about compost, so buy the cheapest – the soil from growbags is an absolute bargain. Then plant in exactly the same way as you did in the garden.

AFTERCARE

Summer bedding plants need a bit of pampering to get the most from them. Regular watering is essential, especially in the early stages when the plants are establishing a root system. In the absence of rain, a thorough watering, twice a week, is generally sufficient for plants in the ground, but those in containers may need a daily soaking if the weather is really hot and dry. Early evening is the best time for this, as less water will evaporate from the compost in cooler night temperatures.

It's also vital to feed regularly – this helps produce healthier plants and lots more flowers, so it's well worth the effort. A once weekly feed of high potash fertiliser

Young plants ready to be potted on.

damage is inevitable when you're splitting them up. Potted plants are the most mature of all, and hence the most expensive, so you might like to compromise by using boxed **cell-grown bedding**. This has proved extremely popular over the past few years, with plants at an intermediate stage between strips and pots. The plants are easy to pop out of the cells and can be planted without any check in growth.

When choosing your bedding plants, avoid any that are dry (they'll feel very light as you pick them up) or potbound (a mass of roots at the base), and certainly don't buy anything that's tall and spindly or has discoloured leaves. Healthy, sturdy, bushy plants are going to do far better in your garden.

Making the most of Geranuims

Geraniums are just about the easiest of all plants to grow so long as you give them a sunny position in well-drained soil. Officially, they should be called pelargoniums, to distinguish them from the true geraniums, which are hardy outdoor plants. They were classified as pelargoniums 200-odd years ago, but it's taking us a while to get used to the idea!

There's a tremendous choice of over 1,000 varieties, in upright and trailing forms. Flower colours range from glorious deep red to the purest of whites, and some varieties even have variegated leaves. The most free-flowering are the seed raised 'Multibloom' varieties, closely followed by the 'zonal' types (those with rounded leaves which often bear a maroon horseshoe marking). Ivy-leaved trailers and the continental 'balcon' varieties, which look so good in large pots, are also very reliable. 'Regal' geraniums (with serrated edges to the leaves) have the showiest flowers, but a much shorter flowering period.

TAKING CUTTINGS

If you want to increase your stocks, geraniums root incredibly easily from cuttings and July is the best time to take them. Choose a healthy plant and, using a sharp knife, cut off a strong shoot about 10cm/4in long, just below a leaf joint. Trim off the lower leaves, and any flowers or flower buds. Insert the cutting to a depth of 2.5cm/1in or so, in a pot of dampened seed and potting compost – a 10cm/4in pot will take up to five cuttings. Keep them on a light windowsill indoors, watering sparingly when the compost begins to dry and they should root within three or four weeks (give a gentle tug to check). They can then be potted into individual 9cm/3¹/₂in pots and left to grow on.

OVERWINTERING

Geraniums aren't hardy, so if you want to keep your plants from year to year, you must bring the pots indoors before the first frost. If they're planted in the ground, lift them with a hand fork, trying not to break off too many roots, and transfer them to pots which are only a little larger than the rootball, filling in any gaps with compost.

Continental 'balcon' geraniums

Leggy plants can be cut back by as much as a half but smaller plants don't need any pruning at all. Stand the pots in a cool light spot indoors, water very infrequently so that the compost is barely moist, and remove any dead leaves. Don't worry if they carry on flowering – leave them to it and enjoy the extra colour. In spring, cut back any woody stems, water more frequently and start to feed. Pinch out the tips of new shoots to encourage good bushy growth and repot if they're growing vigorously, until there's no longer any danger of frost and they can be safely set outdoors.

Geraniums make ideal plants for summer window boxes.

Making the most of Fuchsias

Deservedly amongst the most popular of all bedding plants, there are hundreds of different fuchsias in a wonderful range of colours. Some trail, while others make superb bushes, and most spectacular of all are the tree-shaped 'standards', trained on a single tall stem. The dangling flowers, especially in the double forms, are very glamorous and look particularly lovely against a haze of white or blue lobelia.

Fuchsias dislike hot scorching sun and are happiest in slightly shaded spots. Morning sun is fine, it's the really hot afternoon blaze that can cause problems. They also hate getting too dry, so always keep the soil moist.

TAKING CUTTINGS

Taking cuttings is not only easy, it's a good investment, since fuchsias are one of the more expensive bedding plants. The procedure is exactly the same as for geraniums, except that newly potted cuttings should be kept in a shady spot. Once they begin to grow away strongly, move them to a lighter position and pinch out the tip of the main stem in order to encourage side shoots. In a few weeks, these side shoots will themselves need pinching out in order to develop a good bushy plant.

OVERWINTERING

Unlike their hardy garden cousins (which have rather smaller flowers) bedding fuchsias are tender and need protection from winter weather, but over-wintering them is quite easy and it's well worth the effort. Bring them indoors when frosts threaten, potting them up like geraniums. They need a resting period over winter, so keep them in a cool spot and remove the leaves as they die off. Water very infrequently, just to stop them from getting bone dry.

In spring, encourage them into active growth by first removing them from their pots, shaking off any loose soil and repotting them in fresh compost. They can be cut back to around 5cm/2in from the base (or, in the case of standard fuchsias, cut the head back to 5cm/2in from the stem). Keep the compost moist and spray the wood occasionally with tepid water to get them growing. Once they're growing strongly, pinch out the growing tips to encourage bushing, and water and feed regularly. Plant out when all danger of frosts has passed.

Trailing fuchsias look their best on a garden table or low wall rather than at ground level.

Fuchsia 'Margaret'

(liquid tomato food is excellent, and relatively cheap) really will pay off for both garden and container plants – in our experience, it can help double the number of flowers produced. Delay feeding container plants for five or six weeks, when they will have used up all the plant foods in the fresh compost.

The other weekly chore is dead-heading though, oddly, some people actually enjoy it. Most varieties will do their utmost to produce seed – this diverts the plant's energy from flower to seed production, and it will, after a while, virtually stop flowering. So as soon as you notice fading blooms, pinch them off at the base of the stalk; not only will this tidy up the plant, but it's your insurance policy for next month's flowers.

Spring flowering bedding plants (like pansies, polyanthus and forget-me-nots) are much easier to look after. They're generally planted in autumn and need only the occasional watering if the winter weather has been unusually dry (a rare event indeed). Then as the weather warms up in spring, water them if it's dry, and although they don't need feeding over winter, they'll benefit from a couple of fortnightly feeds in March. And, of course, these bedding plants will need regular dead-heading.

COLOUR AND SCENT

Although it's a matter of personal taste, some colour combinations seem to work whilst others clash dreadfully. As a rule, try to avoid planting mixed colours of different bedding plants together. A mixture of one variety usually looks far better planted with a single colour of another – pastel mixed busy lizzies with silver foliage helichrysum for instance, or white petunias as a soothing foreground for mixed geraniums.

You could, of course, keep it really simple and restrict yourself to just two or three colours. Pale blue, soft pink and white are always effective together, or you could try a really eye-smacking scheme of scarlet and purple. And if you have a really good colour sense, try putting two or three shades of, say, blue together – very brave and, at the moment, very fashionable.

Make the most of winter and spring colour too. In September, garden centres have a good ready-to-plant selection, including wallflowers, pansies, polyanthus and forget-me-nots. Winter-flowering pansies will in fact span both seasons, producing large bright flowers right through the bleakest months, with a final burst of growth in spring. They look wonderful in containers and hanging baskets, or planted in groups of one colour in the garden in spots where they can be seen and admired from the windows. In this way you don't have to venture outside to be able to enjoy their cheerful winter display.

Many bedding plants are sweetly scented, so place them close to doors and windows where you can relish their fragrance which is usually best in the evening. Verbenas are good, and blue or purple petunias can smell as rich as any lily. Best of all, though, are 'Sensation' tobacco plants (nicotiana), which will fill the air with their exquisite fragrance over a very wide area.

A lovely combination of white, soft purples and silver.

Top Ten Bedding Plants

❀ ALYSSUM

One of the most popular, but slightly old fashioned edging plants, producing sweetly scented flowers from mid June to the end of September. Although white is the usual choice, you can find them in rose pink and even apricot. Happiest in sun and a not too heavy soil. In hot summers it is prone to mildew and will stop flowering early. A good garden plant but not recommended for hanging baskets where it struggles to compete with other plants. Height 10cm/4in.

❀ BEGONIA

Colourful and reliable plants for edging, beds, hanging baskets and containers. They're drought-resistant, happy in sun or shade and their only dislike is waterlogged soil. There are two main types. Fibrous rooted (semperflorens) begonias grow 15cm/6in high with attractive bronze or bright green leaves; the pretty flowers are usually red, pink or white. Tuberous varieties are taller (30cm/12in), with larger flowers in a wider range of vibrant colours. These are mostly used for container displays and can be lifted and stored indoors at the end of the season then regrown the following year.

❀ BUSY LIZZIE (Impatiens)

A great favourite. Superb anywhere in the garden and in containers and hanging baskets. Flowers prolifically from a young age all summer (whatever the weather). Happy in sun but is also one of the best for shady spots. A compact plant at 25cm/10in, it's now available in over 20 different colours. New Guinea hybrids are larger (45cm/18in) and combine attractively coloured leaves with terrific flower power; best grown in sun, they look particularly good in containers and can easily be overwintered indoors, treated like geraniums.

❀ LOBELIA

Sold in bush and trailing forms, lobelia can flower from mid June until mid October, as long as the soil doesn't get too dry. It grows best in a fertile soil and sunny position. Both bush and trailing forms are available in white and red as well as the traditional shades of blue. Many gardeners find that the trailing forms get too straggly in hanging baskets and prefer to use the bushy types.

Lobelia

❀ MARGUERITE (Argyranthemum)

A few years ago, the only marguerite widely available was the lovely white flowered Paris daisy. But recently other, very pretty, colours including yellow and pink have been introduced and marguerites are now amongst the most fashionable and showy plants for containers and borders. They are easy to grow in most soils and prefer a sunny position. As tender perennials, they should be brought in for winter and treated like fuchsias. It's also very easy to root them from cuttings in summer.

❀ MARIGOLD (Tagetes)

Anyone can grow them, they flower quickly and whatever variety you've chosen, the display will be bright and longlasting. There are four basic groups. African marigolds are generally taller, with large ball-like flowers, while their cousins, the French marigolds, are shorter and more spreading, with smaller flowers but in larger quantities. Just to confuse us, there is also a group called Afro-French marigolds, combining the dwarfness of the French with the huge double

---

TIPS

✔ *You'll notice at the garden centre or in seed catalogues, that some plants are marked as 'Fleuroselect' award winners. This is a European organization which tests all new seed varieties. Any Fleuroselect variety is good, but a gold award-winner will be superlative.*

✔ *Some bedding plants are labelled as F1 hybrids. These varieties have been specially bred to be more vigorous, and uniform in size, habit and colour.*

✔ *When you're planting bedding in the garden, give the plants a treat by watering them in with liquid tomato food diluted to half strength – it really does get them growing away more quickly.*

flowers of the Africans. Finally, there's the daintiest of the lot, the plants we usually call tagetes, with fine feathery foliage and small single flowers. All are best in sun, in reasonable soil. And all need sunglasses to view them.

✿ PANSY (Viola)

Pansies really cannot be beaten for a magnificent and reliable display of spring colour. Some varieties (like 'Ultima' and 'Universal') flower during the winter as well, although they still peak in spring. The colour range is enormous, from pure white to jet black, and pansies look good anywhere, whether in mixed colours in containers and hanging baskets or in groups of single colours in the border. Good in sun, but especially useful in shade during the spring. For best results, deadhead regularly and water well in dry weather.

✿ PETUNIA

Magnificent plants for sunny spots in borders or containers. Happiest in hot summers, but the newer 'Multiflora' varieties are far more tolerant of wet weather. Don't waste petunias in moist, shady spots – they'll produce plenty of leaves but

very few flowers. Available in lots of colours and in single and (less desirable, we think) double forms. 'Surfinia' varieties are spectacular in hanging baskets, smothered in flower and growing up to ten times the size of traditional varieties. Neatest of all is the new 'Junior' series, with masses of small flowers on compact, bushy plants.

✿ POLYANTHUS

Wonderful spring flowering plants that look like primroses but carry their flowers in clusters. They are also much tougher than most hybrid primroses which garden centres generally sell as indoor plants for cool rooms. Good in containers with dwarf tulips or daffodils, otherwise make a fine front of border plant. Best in moist soil in sun or partial shade, flowering from March to May. Move them immediately after flowering to a shady spot in the garden, to make way for summer bedding.

✿ TOBACCO PLANTS (Nicotiana)

There have been tremendous improvements in breeding over the past few years. The new introductions are superb, compact

Tobacco plants (Nicotiana)

plants, the flowers staying open all day long. These are ideal, undemanding plants for borders and containers and they flower for months (mid June to mid October). Sadly some of these new varieties, such as the excellent 'Domino' series (30cm/12in), have lost the traditional scent, but garden centres still sell the taller growing 'Sensation' varieties (90cm/36in) which are fragrant. Tobacco plants love a good, well drained soil in a sunny spot.

IDEAS FOR LOW-MAINTENANCE

✔ *When planting in the garden, create a slight saucer-shaped dip around each plant. This channels water straight to the rootball and saves both time and water because you can quickly direct the water to the specific plants, rather than watering the whole patch.*

✔ *In a newly planted garden, use bedding plants to fill the gaps between immature shrubs and herbaceous plants. Not only will they look cheerful, but they'll keep the weeds down for you at the same time.*

Marigold

Bulbs

Alliums

Bulbs are one of nature's best conjuring tricks: time bombs, packed with all that's needed for a glorious explosion of flowers. Your only job is to prime the bomb by planting it — the rest happens automatically.

To be pedantic for a moment, some bulbs are technically corms (anemones, for instance), and some are tubers (dahlias), but since they're all to be found in the same section at the garden centre, let's not quibble. The great time for bulbs is the spring spectacular, with daffodils and tulips as the stars, but the show goes on all year round, from winter snowdrops to exotic summer lilies, so make the most of these easy-grow plants.

GROWING SUCCESS

Bulbs are undemanding plants, and very long-lived, but you can help them give of their beautiful best by following a few ground rules.

First, **pick out firm, plump bulbs**, the bigger the better

TWO-TIER PLANTING

Spring bulbs are naturals for containers, and in larger pots and tubs you can double their impact by planting in tiers. It's really quite simple: Using a single variety of daffodil or tulip, follow our guide to planting in containers but set the first layer of bulbs at four times their own depth, leaving a bulb's-width between them. Fill in with compost so that you can just see the 'noses'. Then place the second layer at the normal depth so that they sit between the noses rather than on top of them, and fill in with more compost. The magic of this system is that although the bulbs are at different depths, they will all flower at the same time, making a magnificent display.

A variation on this theme, if you're feeling adventurous, is to use bulbs which flower in succession. One of the best and simplest recipes is to plant tulips in a circle, then use the central area for early crocuses. The crocuses will give the first show, in January and February, with the tulips taking over later.

(more flower power). Reject any that are soft, mildewed or have started to sprout. It's also worth checking the packet to see that they have been commercially grown, rather than collected from the wild.

Then **plant them as soon as possible** – bulbs deteriorate if kept hanging around, especially in a warm room. The only bulb you should delay in planting is the tulip; they're available from August, but it's best to keep them in cool dry conditions and plant in October. This stops them from coming up too early in spring and being harmed by any late hard frosts.

Planting at the correct depth is vital for success, so check the recommended depth on the packet, and stick to it. If you don't, the bulb will rebuke you by failing to flower. As a rule of thumb, if you've no packet to guide you, bulbs should be planted at three times their own depth. Thus a 5cm/2in bulb will need a 15cm/6in hole. Do your best to plant them the right way up (noses skywards), but most will cope if you get it wrong.

In the garden, especially in hard ground, bulb planting can be a bit of a chore, but stick at it. You can

Tulips, daffodils and Anemone blanda *flower brightly at the foot of a tree.*

Making the most of Indoor Bulbs

AMARYLLIS (Hippeastrum)

The amaryllis, with its great strap-shaped leaves and huge trumpet flowers is the most spectacular of all indoor bulbs, and pretty easy to grow.

If you buy yours as a dry bulb, choose the biggest you can find, and pot it up in John Innes No. 2 compost, leaving the top third of the bulb exposed. This is a plant that actually prefers cramped conditions, so make sure that there is only 2.5cm/1in or so of soil between the bulb and the pot. Place in a warm light spot and keep just moist until growth appears, then water more regularly and feed weekly with liquid tomato food.

Amaryllis often keep their leaves right through the year, but sometimes they decide they want a rest. So if the leaves go yellow and die back, just stop watering and keep it dry for two or three months. Gentle watering will then restart it into growth. Repot every two or three years.

HYACINTHS FOR CHRISTMAS

Indoor 'prepared' hyacinths are available in garden centres from August onwards, and it's essential, if you want yours to flower for Christmas, that you plant them by mid September at the latest.

If you're using a bulb bowl or any other container without drainage holes, the best compost is bulb fibre, which stays moist without compacting. Fill the bowl with fibre, then set in the bulbs so that they're almost touching, with their noses just showing. Water gently so that the fibre is moist but not sodden.

Now set the bowl in a shady, cool spot and water as necessary. Once the leaves have emerged and you can just see the flowerspike, move the bowl into a lighter position and let the plants grow on. As soon as the flower buds are ready to open, just bring them into a warm room where they will very quickly develop fully and fill it with their unique perfume.

INDOOR NARCISSI

At the garden centre you'll find a small section devoted to indoor varieties of narcissi. Most of them have a marvellous scent and can flower in as little as six weeks from planting without any special treatment. Just pot them up in the same way as for hyacinths, and leave them in a cool light spot to grow on. And if you want them to look really stunning, tuck in a little primrose plant and add a layer of moss.

Simplest of all, though, are varieties such as 'Paperwhite' and 'Cragford' which will happily grow just in water. A wide glass bowl or jar looks best, and this can be filled with gravel or even small pebbles. Lodge the bulbs in firmly to three-quarters of their depth, then fill up with water to just below the base of the bulbs. All you have to do thereafter is keep the water topped up to this level.

use a trowel to make individual holes, but in soft ground, or after rain, a special bulb planter (which lifts out a plug of soil to the required depth) will be a help. Alternatively you can dig out the whole area, setting the bulbs in at twice their own width apart.

If your soil is heavy or liable to waterlogging, add a 13mm/¹/₂in layer of coarse gravel to the planting hole. This helps drainage and prevents bulbs from rotting.

Once the bulbs are in, fill in with soil, then mark the spot with a short cane or large label. You may think you'll remember where you have planted everything, but you won't.

CONTAINER PLANTING

Planting in containers is much simpler. First make sure that your pot or tub has drainage holes. Then add a layer of gravel or broken crocks to cover the base and prevent the drainage holes from silting up.

Free-draining John Innes No. 2 compost is best for spring bulbs in outdoor containers, while the more moisture-retentive multipurpose composts are fine for summer bulbs like lilies. In large tubs, which would be expensive to fill, you can compromise by replacing just the top few inches with fresh compost.

Set in the bulbs at the recommended depth, spacing them one bulb's-width apart, then fill in with more compost to within 2.5 cm/1 in of the rim and water in. Keep containers watered in warm dry weather, but it shouldn't be necessary to water them in winter.

AFTERCARE

If slugs attack, keep them at bay with slug pellets, or by surrounding the plant with a barrier of ashes, sharp gravel or broken egg shells. Squirrels can sometimes become a problem too, digging up and eating newly planted bulbs. If so, net the area, pinning the net securely in place with short sticks. Once growth appears, the netting can be removed.

Remove faded flowers – if they are allowed to set seed, the bulb will be weakened, and whatever the bulb, leave it to die down naturally after flowering. The energy from the leaves is reabsorbed to form next year's flowers. A high potash feed such as liquid tomato food, after flowering, will also give them a boost.

Over several years, flowering may diminish because the bulbs have increased in number and become overcrowded. Dig them up carefully after flowering, separate them out and replant.

A mix and match planting of dwarf narcissi, crocuses and reticulata irises.

HARMONIOUS PLANTING

Cheerful bulb mixes might seem tempting when planning a spring display, but you'll find that when viewed from a distance your riot of colour has turned into a formless splodge. Bulbs really do look their best and most natural when planted in single colour groups.

That doesn't mean that they can't be teamed up with other bulbs and flowers, but keep it simple. Bluebells and primroses, for instance, relish the same conditions and the soft blues and yellows harmonise beautifully. Or you could use the secret weapon of all spring gardeners – the forget-me-not. The sky-blue flowers, produced right through May, are the perfect accompaniment for late daffodils and tulips. When flowering is over, they're simplicity itself to uproot and discard, leaving a scattering of seedlings for next year's display.

And when you're planting, don't forget the backdrop against which your bulbs will flower. The purple globes of alliums, for instance, look wonderful with pink or white roses, creamy tulips are stunning against a dark green hedge, whilst one of the most magical effects of all can be achieved by underplanting white-stemmed birches with white daffodils.

Top Ten Bulbs

✿ ALLIUM

Brilliant bulbs for early summer, coinciding with the first flush of roses. Showy members of the humble onion family, two favourite varieties are *Allium christophii* with its huge heads of metallic purple stars, and the incredible *Allium giganteum*, whose purple drumstick flowers can tower to 1.8m/6ft. Easy to grow in a sunny, well-drained spot.

✿ ANEMONE BLANDA

One of the delights of March and April, low- growing and needing no special care. The starry flowers of blue, pink or white open out when the sun shines, so it would be

Anemone blanda

PLANTING TIPS

✔ *Make the most of space. There can be quite a large blank area under deciduous shrubs in spring – fill it with bulbs. Once they have flowered, the shrub will be in leaf and obligingly hide their dying foliage.*

✔ *Ideally, buy snowdrops from the garden centre in spring, when they're 'in the green' – ie, uprooted clumps which have just finished flowering. These will establish much more quickly than the tiny dried bulbs you can buy in autumn.*

✔ *Taller varieties of daffodils and tulips are easily damaged by wind, so in exposed spots, use the sturdier short-stemmed varieties.*

✔ *The grape hyacinth,* Muscari armeniacum, *is a pretty little thing, but it's a weed at heart and will self-seed all over the garden. Curb its enthusiasm by planting it in pots only.*

unwise to plant them in a shady spot. Use them in beds, borders, or even in the lawn, where they will naturalise quite easily.

✿ BLUEBELL

These lovely wild flowers increase in number with great enthusiasm, and are best used in wilder parts of the garden, where they can spread freely. They prefer a moist soil, but in fact will grow almost anywhere, in sun or shade. Buy the bulbs early and plant immediately.

✿ CROCUS

One of the earliest bright flowers of the year, with dainty semi-wild varieties in January and February, followed by the larger hybrids in March and April. They can be planted in any sunny, well-drained spot, but look their absolute best when naturalised in the lawn. Sparrows have an unexplained passion for tearing yellow ones to tatters.

✿ DAFFODIL (Narcissus)

The most welcome of spring flowers, giving the first really bold

Bluebells

splash of colour of the year, from as early as February. The range is enormous, with varieties suitable for window boxes, pots, beds, borders and even for naturalising in grass and under trees. Larger varieties like white 'Ice Follies' are commonly called daffodils, while 'narcissus' is generally applied to wild species and smaller hybrids such as 'Tete-a-Tete' and 'February Gold'.

✿ HYACINTH

Because of their delicious perfume, hyacinths are great favourites for growing indoors, but can also be used to give strong blocks of colour in the garden in March and April, interplanted with daffodils or tulips. After the first year, the flowers gradually become more bluebell-like and can be transplanted for naturalising elsewhere in the garden.

✿ IRIS

The early flowering reticulata irises are little gems. They appear in

February, and although they're only 15cm/6in tall, make a real impact. The sky blue 'Joyce' is one of the loveliest, and 'JS Dijt' is the best for scent, but be wary of yellow *Iris danfordiae* which flowers for only one season. Give them a sunny position, in light free-draining soil.

❀ LILY

Of all the summer bulbs, this is the undoubted queen. And despite their exotic looks and fragrance, they're not difficult to grow – the only chore is staking the taller varieties. In the garden, they must have rich well drained soil, but they're perfect for pots, where with good compost and

Snowdrops (Galanthus nivalis)

protection from slugs they'll be magnificent. Start with a beauty like the white *Lilium regale* and you'll be hooked. But do look out for the cherry red lily beetle which is becoming increasingly common in the south – it devastates plants and there's no easy chemical control, so squash it on sight.

❀ SNOWDROP (Galanthus nivalis)

These delicate white flowers are a delight in the dark days of February. They prefer a heavy, moist soil in partial shade, but in fact will grow in all but the driest spots. If clumps become overcrowded, lift them immediately after flowering, tease out the smaller groups of bulbs and replant them.

Lilies make spectacular and long-lasting cut flowers.

IDEAS FOR LOW-MAINTENANCE

✔ Cyclamen hederifolium/neapolitanum *is a wonderful ground cover plant for impossible places. Low growing, with pretty white or pink flowers in late autumn and marbled leaves which persist almost all year, they'll happily increase to make small colonies in dry sunny ground under trees and near hedges. They're most easily established from potted plants rather than dried corms.*

✔ *Most bulbs are perfectly hardy but a few slightly tender varieties, such as dahlias, can be killed over winter in colder areas. Keen gardeners lift them in autumn and clean and store them until spring – not a job for low maintenance gardeners!*

✔ *In wilder areas of the garden, or in grass which is rarely mown, daffodils will naturalise very successfully and grow into substantial drifts. Leave them to seed and spread, without any of the usual dead-heading or annual feeding.*

❀ TULIP

In colour, and in form, this is the most astonishingly varied of all spring bulbs, and if you pick your varieties well you'll have a succession of flower for a full three months. Early varieties include dwarf hybrids such as 'Scarlet Baby' which are perfect for window boxes, while the season ends in May with an explosion of colour from taller types like 'Estelle Rijnveld', one of the outrageously frilled and feathered 'parrot' tulips. But if you want to establish tulips permanently, remember their two essential requirements: a free draining soil, and a sunny south-facing position, where they can enjoy a summer baking.

Climbers and wall shrubs

Climbing plants are invaluable for giving the garden a furnished, settled look and, as a bonus, if you've anything to hide (an ugly wall, a dilapidated shed) they'll do it beautifully.

Clematis flowers

We'll be introducing you to some of the better wall shrubs here, too – plants like ceanothus and pyracantha which will benefit from the warmth and shelter of a wall, and give height and interest. So although they're not climbers, they deserve honorary membership because they too will clothe your walls with style.

GROWING SUCCESS

Climbers are long-lived plants, with a lot of growing to do, so it pays to give them a good start. First, of course, you must choose a healthy plant. Sturdy stems are a good sign but most important of all are the roots. Tip the pot and check the drainage holes – reject any with a mass of roots, but those with just a few roots emerging are at exactly the right stage for planting.

Preparing the planting site is dull work, but vital for success, so don't skimp, especially when you're planting close to walls where the soil is usually poor and dry. It's doubly important when planting a climber to grow up a tree, where it will always face fierce competition from the tree's roots.

First water the plant thoroughly, then dig a hole that's twice the width of the container and 30cm/12in deep. Ideally, set the hole at least 45cm/18in from the wall or tree, though in confined spaces this isn't always possible. Improve the excavated soil by mixing it with equal parts of organic matter such as mushroom compost or well rotted horse manure.

Now carefully tip the plant out of the pot and free any roots which have wound round the rootball. Place the plant in the hole, checking that the surface of the

compost is at ground level, and spread out the loosened roots. Fill in with your soil mix, firming gently as you go and taking care not to leave air pockets. If the stems are not yet long enough to reach the wall, tie them on to angled canes so that they're heading in the right direction. Water well, and keep watered in any dry spells for the next few months.

SUPPORTING

Some climbers, such as ivy and *Hydrangea petiolaris*, are self-supporting, attaching themselves by little aerial roots, so need no help to scale a wall. Most Virginia creepers have special sucker pads on their tendrils. But the twiners (honeysuckle, clematis, wisteria and the like), must have something to hang on to.

A framework of **garden wire** stretched between vine eyes (masonry nails with a hole at the end) is your

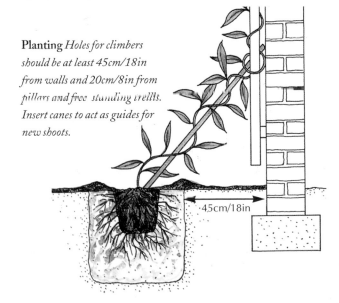

Planting *Holes for climbers should be at least 45cm/18in from walls and 20cm/8in from pillars and free standing trellis. Insert canes to act as guides for new shoots.*

45cm/18in

Making the most of Clematis

Clematis is a treasure amongst climbers, with its glorious blooms, wonderful range of colours and long flowering period.

The large-flowered hybrids are the most immediately attractive, and make a splendid show, most of them growing to no more than a neat 3m/10ft. But small-flowered varieties have their virtues, too. *Clematis montana* makes a dense cover for unsightly walls and garden buildings, and will fling itself up through large trees with reckless abandon, filling them with a mass of blossom in late spring. *Clematis alpina* is much less vigorous (1.8m/6ft) but supremely delicate, with finely cut leaves and nodding spring flowers.

There are just two mysteries attached to clematis. The first is pruning, and we hope that our guidelines will help you there. The second is the dreaded clematis wilt, which plant scientists have had great difficulty explaining. It's a dramatic

Clematis *'Perle d'Azur'*

disease – the plant collapses and dies virtually overnight. Young plants are most susceptible, but a little extra cosseting will help to avoid it.

Most important of all is to plant deeply – 10cm/4in deeper than the plant was in the pot, so that if anything happens to the top growth, there should be dormant underground buds ready to take over. And try to choose a spot where the roots are shaded from the sun – if this is impossible, a large paving slab will help to keep them cool. Then in the first year of growth, keep the plant lavishly watered and give it a monthly feed with any general purpose liquid fertiliser during the summer.

If, despite all your efforts, wilt does strike, cut back all the top growth, and wait – it's quite likely that new growth will spring from the base.

CLEMATIS PRUNING

Clematis differ in their pruning needs, and while it would be

impossible to mention every single variety, this is a breakdown of those you're most likely to find at the garden centre.

No pruning: These smaller-flowered species clematis need no pruning at all, but you can cut them back after flowering if they have outgrown their allotted space: *alpina, armandii, cirrhosa, macropetala, montana, orientalis, tangutica.*

Light pruning: Large-flowered hybrids, flowering in May and June and often again in autumn, need only light pruning in March, just to keep the plant tidy. Barbara Jackman, Bees' Jubilee, Countess of Lovelace, Doctor Ruppel, Duchess of Edinburgh, Elsa Spath, *florida bicolor*, Henryi, Lady Northcliffe, Lasurstern, Lincoln Star, Marie Boisselot, Miss Bateman, Mrs Cholmondeley, Nelly Moser, Richard Pennell, The President, Vyvyan Pennell.

Hard pruning: Summer-flowering varieties, for the most part, which should be cut back hard in February, taking all stems to within 50cm/18in of the ground – sounds drastic, but is essential. Comtesse de Bouchaud, Ernest Markham, Gipsy Queen, Hagley Hybrid, Jackmanii (all), Lady Betty Balfour, Madame Baron Veillard, Madame Edouard Andre, Niobe, Perle d'Azur, Rouge Cardinal, Ville de Lyon, *viticella* (any).

Clematis *'Nelly Moser'*

NORTH WALLS

A sunless wall might seem an inhospitable place for climbers and wall shrubs, but so long as it isn't overshadowed by nearby buildings, a surprising number will thrive.

The all-purpose ivy, in any of the plain green or white- variegated forms, will be perfectly happy, as will that other quietly good-tempered plant, *Euonymus fortunei* 'Silver Queen', a variegated shrub which, rather oddly, turns into a climber if you place it against a wall.

Pyracanthas, too. We tend to associate them with sunny spots, but so long as they're not in a constant draught, they'll enjoy the shelter of the wall and produce a good crop of berries. Winter jasmine (*Jasminum nudiflorum*), with its wands of gold flowers through winter, is another showy plant that does well.

For large expanses of wall, any of the Virginia creepers (*Parthenocissus*) will do nicely. A good even cover, and wonderful autumn colour. And *Hydrangea petiolaris* and *Schizophragma integrifolium* are two further vigorous climbers to treasure for a north wall, with their lacy white flowerheads. Schizophragma isn't easy to find, but well worth tracking down.

And how about clematis? Any number of them flower well in a north-facing position, but just to get you going, take your pick from white 'Marie Boisselot' (exceedingly glamorous), shell-pink 'Hagley Hybrid', mauve-pink 'Nelly Moser', violet 'Vyvyan Pennell' (one of the best of the double-flowered clematis), sky blue 'Perle d'Azur', and deep purple 'Jackmanii' and 'The President'.

cheapest option. The snags are that the wire will sag under a heavy plant if not really taut, and it's going to be very difficult to get to the wall if you want to paint or repair it.

Plastic netting is a good choice for the less vigorous climbers and can be stretched between hooks so that both mesh and plant can be detached and lowered to the ground if you need access to the wall. Bulkier climbers would be safer with a sheet of **rigid plastic mesh**.

Wooden trellis is the most expensive option, but very decorative. Fixing it top and bottom to horizontal battens, using hinges at the bottom and hooks and eyes at the top, allows the whole shooting match to be moved away from the wall if need be. This has the added advantage that the trellis is not flat against the wall and plants can twine in and out quite freely.

TYING IN

Whether your plant is a clinger or a twiner, it will need a little training, to make a good even cover. Tie in new growths with plastic-covered plant ties rather than string (which rots) or wire (which can damage soft stems). Twist the ties so that they're secure, but never knot them – as the stems thicken, a knotted tie can bite in and strangle them, whereas a twisted tie will give.

AFTERCARE

Watering: Climbers on walls or near trees need extra water in warm dry weather, even when they're well established. Give them a thorough soak with a hosepipe, rather than a scattering from the garden sprinkler.

Feeding: A spring feed of rose fertiliser gives all climbers and wall shrubs an annual boost. At the same time, mulch with a layer of well-rotted horse manure to improve the soil, lock in moisture, and keep the weeds down.

Pruning: To keep plants within bounds, and to create a good shape, some pruning is inevitable. Light pruning can be done at any time during the growing season, to any climber or wall shrub (though obviously it would be wiser not to do it when they're in bud or flower), but the rules for more severe pruning differ from plant to plant.

Top Ten Climbers and Wall Shrubs

❀ CEANOTHUS

A mature ceanothus, covered in a mist of blue flowers, is breathtaking. An ideal wall shrub for sun, so long as you have room to accommodate its spreading habit. Of the evergreen varieties, look out for bright blue 'Burkwoodii' (3m/10ft), soft blue 'Autumnal Blue' (3m/10ft) and powder-blue 'Cascade' (3.6m/12ft) – this last has a lovely arching habit. Evergreen ceanothus should never be pruned hard – you risk killing it. Instead, just lightly trim back the sideshoots after flowering.

GROWING TIPS

✔ *People worry about climbers damaging their walls, but there's no need. If the wall is sound to start with, the climber will in fact protect it from the weather and keep it in better condition than an unplanted wall.*

✔ *Be very cautious about planting a Russian vine (Polygonum baldschuanicum). It grows at an astounding speed and will take over your garden, your house, and you, if you stand still for long enough.*

✔ *For a sunny fence or wall, don't forget the annual climbers. Sweet peas are a must (see our section on growing from seed), and other delights include orange* Thunbergia *(black-eyed Susan), sky-blue* Ipomoea *(morning glory) and orange-red* Eccremocarpus *(Chilean glory flower).*

❀ CLEMATIS

The essential climber. The large-flowered hybrids and rampant montana varieties are justifiably popular, but you might like to investigate some of the more unusual members of this remarkable family. The evergreen *Clematis armandii* 'Apple Blossom' is lovely for a sheltered spot – large strap-shaped leaves, and palest pink scented flowers in early spring. *Clematis tangutica* and *C. orientalis* have ferny leaves and small bell-shaped blooms in bright yellow, produced from August to October.

❀ HEDERA (Ivy)

One of the most adaptable of all climbers, with a terrific variety of leaf form and colour. The golden forms are great for a sunny spot – the enormous green/gold leaves of 'Sulphur Heart' for instance (also known as 'Paddy's Pride'), or the daintier 'Buttercup', which is entirely gold in full sun. A good tip on speed of growth is that in general, large-leaved forms are

Jasminum nudiflorum

Hydrangea petiolaris

more vigorous than small-leaved, and that plain green varieties put on more of a sprint than the variegated ones. Ivies can be pruned as hard as you like in spring.

❀ HYDRANGEA PETIOLARIS (Climbing hydrangea)

Slow to establish, but once it gets going, this self-clinging climber can soar to 15m/50ft, covered in large white lacecap flowers in June. Those of a nervous disposition might like to try one of its close relatives, *Schizophragma integrifolium*, which will reach a mere 9m/30ft. The midsummer flowers are interesting – an inner circle of tiny florets, surrounded by dangling white bracts. Neither plant needs regular pruning, but can be tidied up after flowering.

❀ JASMINUM NUDIFLORUM (Winter jasmine)

With its bright yellow flowers from November to spring, this is an invaluable shrub (to 3m/10ft) for a north facing position, but will also thrive in a sunny spot. The long whippy stems should be tied in to a support and allowed to cascade forward. Prune after flowering, thinning out a few of the older stems to encourage new growth.

❀ LONICERA (Honeysuckle)

Valued for their incomparable scent, honeysuckles like an airy position in sun or partial shade. They twine, and need support on a wall, but will happily scramble freestyle up trees. Two of the showiest are May/June flowering 'Belgica', and 'Serotina', flowering July to October. Both grow to 4.5m/15ft or more. The more vigorous semi-evergreen 'Halliana' has simpler white/cream blooms, but flowers non-stop from mid-summer to late autumn. Lightly prune after flowering, and thin out some of the older stems. If plants become hopelessly tangled and scrawny-looking, cut right back to the main stems in March.

❀ PARTHENOCISSUS

All the plants in this group, including Virginia creeper, are excellent for covering a vast expanse, very quickly. They're self-clinging and have the charming habit, when no wall-space remains, of draping down in great festoons. The autumn colour is spectacular. *Parthenocissus tricuspidata* 'Veitchii' (Boston ivy), is one of the best, for its glossy apple-green leaves and neat uniform growth, to 15m/50ft. No pruning needed, but can be cut back in spring if necessary.

❀ PYRACANTHA (Firethorn)

An excellent wall shrub for sun, with glossy evergreen leaves and small white flowers followed by red, orange or gold berries. 'Orange Glow' is especially good. To keep them flat to the wall, they need to be firmly attached. The long shoots can be cut back after flowering (wear gloves – the spines are vicious) to keep the plant compact. They grow

Solanum crispum *'Glasnevin'*

Pyracantha

to around 3m/10ft, with a similar spread, but can be cut to shape to make a formal feature (round a door, for instance), though this inevitably limits flowering and berrying.

❀ SOLANUM CRISPUM 'GLASNEVIN' (Chilean potato tree)

A scrambling wall shrub for a sunny spot, with large heads of blue-purple flowers right through summer. 6m/20ft. Easy to please, but rather lax growth, so looks better when trained in to a wall. Prune in April, taking out old or damaged growths and shortening any stragglers. The white *Solanum jasminoides* 'Alba' is very similar, but not quite so hardy.

❀ WISTERIA

The classic climber, with a spectacular early summer waterfall of flowers, but must have a south or west wall. Try to buy grafted plants – cheaper seed-raised plants can take up to 12 years to flower. And check the eventual height before you buy; *Wisteria sinensis* can reach 30m/100ft, while *Wisteria floribunda* grows to a much more manageable 9m/30ft. A solid,

woody plant, wisteria needs very firm wall support, and a pruning regime is essential for good flowering. In July, cut back all sideshoots (there will be plenty) to around 15cm/6in, leaving six buds. In February, reduce these same shoots by a further 5cm/2in or so, so that only two or three buds remain.

Container gardening

Ring the changes by surrounding permanent plants like this phormium with cheery seasonal bedding.

Virtually anything can be grown in containers, from colourful bedding plants and tasty vegetables to scented climbers, even small trees. And virtually anything can be used as a container, from old shoes and paint cans to the more traditional terracotta pots and wooden barrels.

The other great thing is that you're making the most of all available space – cramming a balcony, brightening up a gloomy corner, cheering up a plantless patio. You can even shuffle the pots around for an instant change of scene.

Container plants do need a little more care than those in the open ground, but this form of 'gardening in miniature' gives you tremendous scope for change and for some really exquisite effects.

GROWING SUCCESS
SOIL
It really is important to use good compost. Resist the temptation to save money by using garden soil; it's not the right consistency for container gardening and it can harbour pests and diseases, so your plants will inevitably struggle.

For shrubs, climbers or trees, which are likely to remain in the same container for several years, use a soil-based John Innes No. 2 or No. 3 compost. Herbs and bulbs, too, will appreciate the sharp drainage that this type of compost provides.

Peat-based composts, often labelled as 'multipurpose', are ideal for bedding plants, vegetables or anything that's being planted for just a few months. Growbag compost, decanted into containers, is the cheapest option of all.

Ericaceous composts are specially formulated for acid-loving plants such as rhododendrons, azaleas, camellias and pieris.

DRAINAGE
Whatever container you're using, it's essential that it's well drained to prevent waterlogging. So check that it has drainage holes – most do, but some, like wooden barrels, have solid bases. If this is the case you'll have to get drilling (five well spaced 13mm/^{1}/$_2$in holes would be ideal in this instance).

The other golden rule is to add drainage material to the base of the container. This prevents compost from being washed away when you water, and from blocking up the drainage holes. Broken clay pots

Winter-flowering pansies put on a final great burst in spring.

PLANTING FOR A SHADY SITE

Provided it's not cast in perpetual gloom, any shady paved area that catches just a little sun can become home to a remarkable variety of plants in pots. Many summer bedding plants, such as **fuchsias** and **busy lizzies**, will flourish, but it's the leafy plants that really furnish a shady spot.

Ferns are naturals for this sort of situation. All too often they look wispy and uninviting at the garden centre, but they can grow into quite magnificent plants. Evergreen varieties with light green fronds are perfect, one of the best being the soft shield fern, *Polystichum setiferum*.

Hostas will love it too, so exploit all their colours from blue-grey to white-variegated, and their sculptural leaf shapes.

Ground cover **lamiums** can be tamed in pots and are ideal for shade, especially the white or silver-variegated forms, though it would be best to shear them over now and again to keep them compact. And that other rampant plant, **helxine** (mind-your-own- business: hardy, but usually sold as a houseplant), makes a beautiful green cushion of tiny leaves in a pot – but never let it anywhere near a piece of open ground!

Pieris will give you a cascade of evergreen foliage with the bonus of spring flowers and flaming red young shoots, and **Japanese acers** will provide the icing on the cake. Expensive, and slow-growing, but they're exquisite small trees for pots. The cut-leaved varieties, whether plain green or plum-purple, are the most delightful of all.

That's rather a 'Japanese garden' sort of picture we've painted – leafy and quiet – but if you want to jazz it up, add in some camellias, azaleas, rhododendrons, hydrangeas and a few gold- variegated shrubs.

(crocks) or little stones are ideal for smaller containers and broken bricks can be used in larger ones. Don't skimp on it; a 2.5-5cm/1-2in layer in medium to large pots and up to 15cm/6in in the very largest barrels.

PLANTING
After adding the drainage material, fill in with compost to within 2.5cm/1in or so of the rim of the container, firming it down but not squashing it. Using a hand trowel, dig individual holes for each of the plants, taking care that they're set in at the same level as they were in the original pot. Gently firm the compost around them, adding more if needed. Water thoroughly until you see the excess running out of the bottom of the container.

WATERING
From then on, the amount of watering required depends on the time of year and position of the container (if it's in a sunny spot, it will need more watering than one in shade). You'll also find that larger containers dry out less quickly than smaller ones, and that plastic pots need less water than terracotta.

The most difficult thing is to tell whether to water or not. The simple answer is to check each container regularly in the summer – put your finger into the compost and if it feels dry more than 2.5cm/1in beneath the surface then it needs watering. In sunny positions, smaller pots could need daily watering and larger ones up to three times a week. For the rest of the year it's

Trailing or low-growing plants such as this viola can be used to soften the edges of your container planting.

much simpler – a weekly check should be sufficient. By the way, don't assume that if it's been raining your pots will have been well watered. Dense foliage can deflect the rain and even after a heavy shower the compost could still be dry.

FEEDING
Four or five weeks after planting, the fertiliser in the compost will be running out. Seasonal plants – fruit, vegetables and summer bedding – are greedy, and will need a weekly feed of high potash fertiliser such as liquid tomato food thereafter. Permanent plants need

only two feeds of a general purpose fertiliser such as Phostrogen – one in late March and the second in late June. Feeding is important for the health of the plants; in the garden their roots can go exploring for food, but in a container they have to rely on you to do the catering.

REPOTTING

Strong-growing plants such as trees or shrubs will occasionally need repotting into larger containers, and usually let you know by growing much less vigorously. Water them well, wait an hour, then remove them and place in the new pot, filling in with fresh compost.

TOPPING UP

When plants reach maturity and are permanently settled, it's a good idea to freshen the compost each year by removing the top 5-10cm/2- 4in in spring and adding a layer of new compost.

CREATING A BOX BALL

Evergreen box *(Buxus)* is one of the easiest of all shrubs to train into a decorative shape. Pinch out all the growing tips of the young plant to encourage bushing, then trim regularly but lightly to shape it up. Pot on as it grows – once mature, it will need only an occasional haircut with the shears.

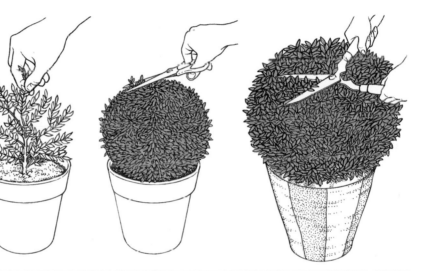

DECORATIVE TERRACOTTA

Terracotta pots are our number one favourites when it comes to containers. The sturdy simplicity of the plain flowerpot type is always pleasing, but there are some wonderfully decorative pots available direct from the potteries and from garden centres.

Pie crust pots have a crimped edge, and the smaller ones look especially pretty planted up with simple flowers like primroses which echo the pot's wavy rim. Pastry pots are decorated with twisted ribbons of clay. Onion pots are delightfully squat and fat-bellied.

Fanciest (and most expensive) of all are the Italianate pots – a riot of swags and garlands, which look most effective if you use them for just one striking plant. Or put in two or three plants of one colour and variety; an Italian pot planted with pink continental 'balcony' geraniums will be a show-stopper all summer.

Some pots are so handsome that they don't need to be planted at all. Curvy ali baba jars, wide-shouldered Greek oil jars, and bell-shaped rhubarb forcers can look wonderful set in the border, or used as a focal point for a favourite planting.

Terracotta looks better the older it gets, and antique pots command premium prices because of the patina of age they have acquired. But a brand new pot can be 'aged' within months rather than years if you brush it with dilute fertiliser or yoghurt – it'll soon take on that soft, weathered look.

Making the most of your Container

As we said earlier, virtually anything that holds compost can be used as a plant container, but when you've run through your supplies of old shoes, paint cans and mop buckets, it could be time for a trip to the garden centre to stock up with something more conventional.

Terracotta pots, plain or fancy, are the most desirable of all containers. They're heavy and stable and their natural warm colour complements all plants, particularly as they mellow with age. The downside is that they can be expensive, are breakable and can shatter in frost unless you buy the higher-quality pots which are guaranteed frost-proof. They're also porous, so need watering more frequently in summer. But their ability to blend so happily into the garden scene far outweighs these few disadvantages.

OTHER MATERIALS

Plastic containers are inexpensive and long-lasting. Available in many colours to suit most situations, they withstand frost and are easy to clean. And they're light, which is useful in places like balconies where weight is important. However, the cheaper pots can become brittle in sunlight and may need replacing after a year or so. Synthetic materials are also used to make imitation terracotta pots, and some are pretty convincing.

Wooden tubs and **half-barrels** are good value but should be treated with timber preservative to prevent rotting. As an additional precaution against decay, it helps if you line the inside with polythene (but do make

Petunias, daisies and helichrysum bask in a fluted terracotta pot, backed by pink nicotianas.

some holes in the bottom so that water can still drain away).

Glazed pots are becoming increasingly popular, partly because they tend to be cheaper than terracotta. They are frost resistant and usually sold with a matching saucer which can be useful when watering. Single colours (especially the blue) are lovely, but some of the more hectic designs can be (how can we put this nicely?) distracting.

Fibre containers have a peat-like texture and are relatively cheap. However they will gradually degrade and usually only last a couple of years.

Growbags are one of the cheapest and easiest ways of container gardening. Most people use them to grow tomatoes, but you can get excellent results with many other plants, including flowers,

herbs and strawberries. The bags are somewhat garish, but can be disguised by planting a couple of quick growing trailing plants (lobelia or dwarf nasturtium for instance) around the edge. They can also dry out quickly, so keep a careful eye on watering.

You can even re-use them in the second year. If you've grown tomatoes in them in the first season, remove the larger roots, fluff up the compost and grow French beans, herbs, strawberries or bedding plants. And at the end of the season, chuck the twice-used compost on the garden as a soil improver. Growbags really are great value for money!

Top Plants for Container Gardening

❧ BEDDING PLANTS

Top performers for summer include marguerites, dwarf nicotiana, verbena, geraniums and fuchsias. For contrast, add in attractive foliage plants like silver-leaved *Senecio maritima* and helichrysum, or ferny-leaved Swan River daisy (brachycome). Later colour can be provided by the remarkable winter flowering pansies which put on a final great burst in spring. And polyanthus looks especially good in smaller pots early in the year. The keys to success with all these plants are constant removal of spent flowers and, in summer, regular watering and feeding.

❧ BULBS

You can create a terrific long-lasting spring display by planting up a number of pots, each with a different variety; say, species *Crocus* 'Snowbunting' which flowers in February, dwarf *Narcissus* 'Quail' for March colour, while in late April one of the best varieties is the dwarf tulip, 'Red Riding Hood'. For summer colour, grow blue or white agapanthus which thrive in sunny spots. And lilies are magnificent and easy to grow (for a real show, plant three bulbs in a 25cm/10in pot).

A spring planting of daffodils, tulips hyacinths and muscari.

❀ CLIMBERS

All but the most vigorous climbers are happy in containers. Large-flowered clematis are excellent, as are honeysuckles, summer and winter jasmine, and the colourful variegated ivies. Annual climbers such as black-eyed Susan (thunbergia) and morning glory (ipomoea) are fast growing and eye-catching choices for pots in sunny spots. For perennial climbers, choose a pot big enough for at least two years' growth – if you find this hard to estimate, check with a plant expert at your garden centre.

❀ FRUIT

It often surprises people that fruit can be grown in pots. Top fruit (tree fruit such as apples) needs large pots, up to half-barrel size. A dwarfing rootstock is essential – M27 for apples, 'Pixy' for plums, 'Colt' for cherries. Few of the soft fruit varieties are happy in containers, though red, white and blackcurrants do well. Without doubt, the most successful of all are strawberries which not only look good but give excellent crops. Plant either singly in 10cm/4in pots or in special strawberry pots with side planting holes. All fruit needs to be grown in a sunny position.

❀ HERBS

Herbs grow well in containers and are particularly rewarding – they're troublefree, grow quickly, look good together and smell wonderful. Some, like thyme, marjoram and sage, are available in golden and variegated forms and can be used very effectively to contrast with other plants. Shaped bay looks magnificent in pots, but needs winter protection in colder areas. Most herbs are happiest in sunny spots and can put up with a bit of drought (when you or God forget to water them). Mint is the main exception, needing to be kept moist, so place a saucer under the

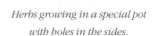

Clematis trained to climb up a wigwam of canes.

Herbs growing in a special pot with holes in the sides.

pot and keep it topped up with water in summer.

❀ ROSES

Many modern roses have been bred for compact bushy growth and almost continuous flower, making them ideal for pots. Patio roses, in particular, are superb. They are larger and more robust versions of miniature roses, with charming flowers and a neat growth habit. One of the best is apricot-peach 'Sweet Dream' (45cm/18in). Climbing roses can be extremely vigorous, so search out shorter varieties like the 2.4m/8ft 'Golden Showers'. To thrive, container-grown roses need a reasonably sunny spot and a feed with rose fertiliser twice a year, in late March and late June. The one disadvantage is that they can look so dull in winter, so tuck in a few small plants such as variegated ivies to lighten the gloom.

❀ SHRUBS

Some of the most useful shrubs are those that look good all year round. Flowering evergreens like camellias,

Rhododendron yakushimanum

rhododendrons, choisya and winter-flowering *Viburnum tinus* 'Eve Price' are good choices. Some evergreens are grown purely for their attractive foliage and huge-leaved *Fatsia japonica*, spiky phormiums and cordylines (both slightly tender) and many conifers are worth considering. In shadier spots, try any of the gold-spotted laurels (aucuba) or *Euonymus fortunei* 'Emerald 'n' Gold', one of the finest golden variegated dwarf evergreens.

❀ TREES

Nothing else provides such a dramatic instant effect and any of the smaller trees can be grown very successfully in larger tubs. Cut-leaved Japanese maples (*Acer palmatum* varieties) are particularly choice in shade, while weeping *Cotoneaster salicifolius* 'Pendulus' is good in sun. For flower, crab apples (*Malus*) must come top of the

list – 'Red Jade' is one of the very best, with white spring blossom followed by abundant red fruit. Be bold – any tree that takes your eye and grows to around 3.6m/12ft will be perfectly happy in a large tub or half-barrel.

❀ VEGETABLES

Vegetables in containers can look surprisingly decorative – courgettes, for instance, have beautiful leaves. The most rewarding are those that yield the biggest crop from the smallest area – climbing plants like runner beans, mangetout or sugar peas, and fast-maturing plants like lettuce and radishes. Tomatoes are great, especially the tasty cherry-sized 'Gardener's Delight' and 'Sungold', with bumper crops even in a 25cm/10in pot.

Peppers in growbags.

Fruit

A succulent sun-warmed strawberry, a sweet, ripe pear dripping juice down your chin, a crisp, rosy apple fresh from the tree; all it takes to grow fruit is a finely-tuned set of taste buds, and a little annual care.

Victoria plum

Fruit trees and bushes can be very beautiful in their own right – apple blossom in spring, fruit-laden trees in autumn, the gleam of fat bunches of blackcurrants and the translucent globes of gooseberries. A feast for the eye as well as the stomach. The fruits we recommend here are all on our 'easy' list – those that you can grow with a minimum of fuss and maximum crops. Have a go. It's tremendously satisfying.

GROWING SUCCESS

Most fruit needs a sunny spot, though raspberries, currants and gooseberries will tolerate some shade.

Producing crops year after year is hard work, so give your plants the best possible start by enriching the soil with generous quantities of well rotted horse manure or other organic material.

Plant container grown fruit at the same level as it was in the pot, and bare-root plants (available during the dormant season) with the junction of stem and roots just below ground level (there will be a dark soil mark to guide you), spreading the roots as widely as possible.

Water plants regularly during their first summer; in future years, tree fruits benefit greatly from a thorough watering during prolonged dry spells. Feed with a high

Strawberries are one of the easiest fruits to grow successfully, even in the smallest garden. The heaviest crops are produced in the first few years, so scrap your plants once fruiting starts to diminish, and replace with fresh stocks.

potash fertiliser such as rose food in spring, and add a mulch of organic matter like compost or well rotted manure to keep the soil in good condition.

Pruning varies according to the type of fruit, and we have advocated the simplest possible methods for each one. One important tip – always cut just above an outward facing sideshoot or bud.

If you grow and look after your fruit well, serious problems are unlikely. The commonest are covered in the chapter on pests and diseases (see page 89), but where a problem is specific to a particular fruit, you'll find it described here.

CREATE A FEATURE

Mature apple and pear trees, with their dark, gnarled branches, have great dignity and presence in the garden, and can easily be one of its most striking features.

Enhance them even further by using them as a support for a climbing plant such as a rose or clematis. But do a little homework first. Choose a climber that won't swamp the tree, but will politely ramble through it to a reasonable height. And when selecting clematis, opt for summer- rather than spring-flowering varieties. They'll take over when the tree's blossom is just a happy memory.

An espalier pear tree, trained against a wall.

WELL-TRAINED FRUIT

Sounds tricky? Not at all – training fruit trees, especially into cordons or espaliers, is a brilliant way of saving space and not nearly so difficult as you might think.

Cordon apples and pears are grown on a single unbranched stem against a wall or fence. Buy a pre-trained tree and plant it at an angle of around 45°, secured to a bamboo cane – several trees set 90cm/3ft apart look especially effective and you can do a mix and match of varieties that cross-pollinate. Prune each August, first cutting back any brand new shoots from the main stem to 7.5cm/3in. Then turn your attention to the shoots that were pruned last year – they will have formed smaller sideshoots which should be pruned back to 2.5cm/1in. And that's it! You've just trained a fruit tree.

Espaliers are a kind of living fence, with three or more matching pairs of branches trained horizontally from the main stem. Again, start with a pre-trained tree, tie it in to wires, and prune it in the same way as cordons. Espaliers can be grown against walls or fences, or as a fruitful boundary between one part of the garden and another.

Once you get the bug for trained trees, you might want to have a go at other forms, like fans, pyramids and even step-overs (low-growing mini-fences). If you do, seek guidance from the RHS's *The Fruit Garden Displayed* – it's the committed fruit-grower's bible.

SELECTING FRUIT FOR THE SMALL GARDEN

In tiny gardens, fruit might seem like a luxury, but there are plenty of ways of tucking in a few plants for that unique fresh-picked flavour.

Strawberries grow well in pots and, even better, in hanging baskets, where they'll be safe from even the most athletic slug. Raspberries can be set along a fence, blackberries and loganberries trained against a wall.

Dwarf apples take up very little space – those on the smallest rootstocks do well in a large pot or half-barrel. Gooseberries and blackcurrants will also thrive in pots or tubs, and you can have fun creating a gooseberry 'tree' by training it on a single stem, taking out all the side shoots as they emerge and leaving the top growth to bush out.

And don't overlook the ornamental value of tree fruits. Crab apples *(Malus)*, for instance, are beautiful small trees in their own right, with a wealth of spring blossom, and masses of brightly coloured fruit in autumn which makes a delicious jelly.

Apple and pear minarettes make an ideal choice for the small garden.

Essential Fruit Facts

Apple 'Sunset'

❀ APPLES

For good crops you need two compatible varieties which will cross-pollinate, and garden centres and fruit growers have charts to help you. One of the few exceptions is the new self-fertile Cox's Orange Pippin which can be grown on its own.

Trees on dwarfing rootstocks are best for small gardens, and the approximate mature heights for these is:

M27	1.5m/5ft
M9	2.4m/8ft
M26	3m/10ft
MM106	3.6m/12ft

Apples need a warm sheltered spot, planted at a distance apart that equals their mature height. The tiniest trees, on M27 and M9, need a rich soil to do well and because the roots lack vigour, should be staked all their lives to keep them firmly anchored. Other rootstocks need only be staked (to 60cm/2ft) for the first two or three years.

Pruning is largely a matter of common sense, and although there are special techniques to encourage extra fruiting, a well-shaped healthy tree will naturally crop well. The aim is to create an open, goblet shape, so that all parts of the tree receive their fair share of air and sunshine.

In the first winter after planting, take out the leading stem, leaving three or four well-spaced sideshoots which should be cut back by two-thirds at this stage – they will eventually become the main branches. By the following winter, they will have thickened and produced their own sideshoots. Cut back the long new growths of these branches by half, and do the same to the sideshoots (removing any that are congested or cross the centre of the tree).

Thereafter, remove any vigorous upright stems in summer, and keep the tree trimmed to shape in winter, shortening long whippy stems and removing crossing or weak growths. A few varieties, such as 'Discovery' and 'Worcester Pearmain', bear fruit only at the tips of the branches, so if yours does this, prune out a third of the fruited shoots each winter, to encourage fresh growth.

Remove any fruits in the first summer, to build up a strong tree.

Troubleshooting

Brown rot, with concentric rings of white mould, is caused by a fungus entering damaged fruit. Remove and destroy affected apples.

Bitter pit causes brown flecking of skin and flesh, and a bitter flavour. It is most prevalent after a hot dry summer, so water thoroughly in any dry spells.

Scab appears as brown woody patches, and is worst in humid weather and on congested trees. Prune to keep the tree open, and destroy any affected fruits and fallen leaves. The caterpillars of the **codling moth** feed inside the apple, and tunnel their way out when the fruit is ripe. Hang pheremone traps in the trees from late spring, to lure the male moths before mating begins.

Woolly aphids on stems and trunks cover themselves in a fluffy white 'cotton wool'. They do no great harm and can simply be washed off with the hose.

Recommended varieties

Eating: Egremont Russet, Fortune (Laxton's Fortune), Sunset.
Cooking: Bramley's Seedling, Grenadier.

❀ BLACKBERRIES

Blackberries are long-lived, easy plants, and can tolerate some shade. Support the rambling canes (stems) on a framework of four or five wires stretched between posts, to a height of around 1.8m/6ft. One exception is the non-rambling 'Loch Ness' which can be grown in the same way as raspberries.

Blackberry 'Loch Ness'

GROWING TIPS

✔ *Peaches are tricky to grow in the garden, needing a lot of extra cosseting. But you might like to try the new dwarf 'patio' peaches, in a sunny spot. Bring them in to a light, cool room from late autumn to the end of May, to protect them from frost and from the wet weather which can spread peach leaf curl on the young leaves.*

✔ *Fruit trees are sometimes planted as a centrepiece in a lawn. Always leave a 90cm/3ft circle of bare soil around the trunk, to allow for annual mulching and prevent grass from competing for water and nutrients.*

After planting, cut any canes back to 30cm/12in. In the first summer, new canes should be trained along the wires, to fruit the following summer. After fruiting, cut them back to ground level and tie in the new set of canes.

Loganberries, with larger, cylindrical fruits, are closely related, and can be grown in exactly the same way.

Troubleshooting
Blackberries are healthy plants and not prone to any particular pests or diseases.

Recommended varieties
Fantasia, Loch Ness, Merton Thornless, Oregon Thornless.

❀ BLACKCURRANTS
Blackcurrants like a sheltered spot with moisture-retentive soil, in sun or partial shade, and should be spaced 1.5m/5ft apart.

In the first winter, cut stems back almost to soil level, so that only one bud is visible. In the second winter, take out any weak or crossing growth. The following summer they will fruit, and the simplest method of

pruning once they are fully established is to take out a quarter of the oldest branches to the base, immediately after fruiting. This ensures a constant supply of new fruiting wood.

Troubleshooting
Big bud is caused by a gall mite and is most evident in winter, with some buds much larger and rounder than normal. Pick off and burn them. Serious infestations can cause a virus which drastically reduces crops, and these plants should be destroyed.

Recommended varieties
Ben Lomond, Ben Sarek, Boskoop Giant, Wellington XXX

❀ GOOSEBERRIES
Gooseberries are old favourites for pies and jellies, but the eating varieties, bursting with juice and sweetness, are excellent too.

Space plants 1.5m/5ft apart in a sunny spot. In the first winter, cut out any low-growing shoots, leaving a 15cm/6in 'trunk', and prune the remaining stems back by half. In following winters, remove a few older and crossing branches to keep the centre of the bush open and stimulate new growth.

Troubleshooting
Gooseberry sawfly is a caterpillar which strips the leaves in an alarmingly short time. Remove by

Gooseberry 'Careless'

Pear 'Doyenne du Comice'

hand, or spray with malathion.

Recommended varieties
Careless (green, cooking), Invicta (green, cooking), Leveller (green, eating), Whinham's Industry (red, eating and cooking).

❀ PEARS
Eating a ripe pear can be a messy business, but they're so delicious that you can be excused for forgetting your table manners. But they do need a warm climate and sheltered, sunny position to do well, and can be difficult to grow in colder regions. And as with apples, you'll need two varieties for cross-pollination.

The two available dwarfing rootstocks are 'Quince C' (approx. 2.1m/7ft) and 'Quince A' (approx. 3m/10ft). Staking, training and pruning can be undertaken in the same way as apples.

Troubleshooting
Scab and **brown rot** should be dealt with as described for apples.
Pear midge lays eggs on flowers and the ensuing maggots cause immature fruits to blacken and fall. Collect and destroy the fruits to help prevent maggots returning to the soil to pupate.

Recommended varieties
Beth, Beurre Hardy, Conference, Doyenne du Comice, Williams' Bon Chretien.

❀ PLUMS

The natural vigour of plums can be cut down to size with a dwarfing rootstock. 'St Julien A' restricts them to around 3.6m/12ft, and 'Pixy' to a mere 2.4m/8ft or so. However, the fruit from a tree grown on 'Pixy' rootstock does tend to be smaller than normal.

Plums flower very early, so plant in a warm sheltered spot where there is least likelihood of frost damage to the flowers. Some plums need another tree for cross-pollination, but those recommended here are self-fertile and can be grown singly. The eating varieties, especially 'Ouillins Gage' and 'Imperial Gage' have a superb, honeyed flavour.

Stake plums as described for apples. No routine pruning is needed, but you can train the tree as it grows, taking out any weak or crossing growths to keep the centre open. Always prune in early summer, to reduce the risk of silver leaf disease.

Troubleshooting

Silver leaf is a highly destructive fungus which enters through wounds or pruning cuts. It causes a silvery sheen on leaves and a brown central staining in infected branches. Remove and destroy affected wood, cutting back to healthy unstained wood. This should be done in the summer months and the pruning cuts painted with a wound sealant such as Arbrex. The much commoner '**false silver leaf**' produces similar syptoms but does not stain the wood, and is harmless.

Recommended varieties

(All self-fertile) Czar (cooking), Imperial Gage, also known as Denniston's Superb (eating), Marjorie's Seedling (cooking), Ouillins Gage (eating), Victoria (eating and cooking).

❀ RASPBERRIES

Raspberries need a rich moist soil in sun or partial shade. To support the canes, stretch two or three strands of wire between posts, to a height of 1.5m5ft. Set plants 45cm/18in apart and prune each cane to within 25cm/10in of the ground.

Raspberry 'Leo'

Next spring and summer, tie in new canes as they grow. These canes produce fruit the following summer, after which they should be cut back to ground level and fresh canes tied in. Autumn fruiting varieties such as 'Autumn Bliss' and 'Zeva' are an exception – all their canes should be cut back in February.

Troubleshooting

Raspberry beetle larvae can infest the fruit. If they are active in your area, spray with malathion when the first berries begin to ripen.

Recommended varieties

Autumn Bliss, Glen Moy, Leo, Malling Admiral, Malling Jewel.

❀ STRAWBERRIES

Strawberries are the most eagerly anticipated of summer fruits. They need a warm sunny site that has been generously enriched with well rotted manure. In pots, tubs and hanging baskets, use fresh multipurpose compost.

Set plants 40cm/15in apart, leaving 75cm/30in between rows, with the base of the 'crown' (the point from which top growth starts) just below ground level.

In summer, plantlets are formed on long runners, and these should be removed. Fruits can be protected from soil-splash and (to a certain extent) slugs by laying clean dry straw or special strawberry mats under them. After fruiting, remove any remaining runners, and cut off the older, larger leaves.

Strawberries can crop for three to six years. Scrap them once they begin to lose vigour, though you can allow a few runners to root to create a fresh stock of plants. Choose a new planting site, and start all over again.

Troubleshooting

Apart from slugs and botrytis (see Pests and Diseases), strawberries are very susceptible to viruses. Symptoms vary, but fruiting will deteriorate and as there's no cure, plants should be removed and destroyed.

Recommended varieties

Aromel, Honeoye, Mara des Bois, Symphony, Tenira.

IDEAS FOR LOW-MAINTENANCE

✔ *Ballerina and minerette apples grow on a single unbranched stem, and need little pruning. They do very occasionally produce a branch, but this can easily be nipped off.*

✔ *Alpine strawberries make very pretty ground cover plants and are especially useful in shady spots. The tiny berries are highly flavoured and you should be able to pick a small handful each day in high summer. The most widely available variety is 'Baron Solemacher'.*

Garden planning and design

Don't let the title put you off. Planning and design is nothing grand – it's simply a matter of making the most of your garden's potential, whether you're starting from scratch, taking over an existing garden or just want to revamp the one you've had for years.

It's a bit like planning to furnish and decorate a room – though in this case the room will actually improve over the years. And as long as you apply a few common-sense rules, you'll end up with a garden that's exactly right for you.

STARTING FROM SCRATCH
INITIAL PLANNING

Starting with a blank canvas (a garden attached to a brand new house, or a totally neglected, weed-infested plot) is the most exciting challenge of all – your chance to transform one small piece of Mother Earth.

First sit down and think what you want from your garden. If you have a young family, it's important to allow for a safe playing area such as a lawn, to use tough plants that will survive footballs and games of hide-and-seek, and to avoid potentially dangerous features like a pond or pool. Do you also want to use it for entertaining family and friends? If so, you'll need a flat paved area that will comfortably accommodate the garden furniture (and the barbecue), and the chances are that you'll want this to be in the sunniest part of the garden to make the most of warm weather.

How much time do you want to spend working in your garden? Is it for pure relaxation or will you enjoy spending a few hours or more a week working in it? The reason for thinking about this so early in the planning stage is that it helps decide how much space to allocate

A strong, simple design is often the most effective. Dwarf box hedges give this hard-surfaced front garden its structure.

to different types of plants. Trees, shrubs and herbaceous plants, for example, need very little looking after, while a large vegetable plot can be extremely time-consuming.

Finally, consider how much money you want to spend. Generally, hard landscaping features (like paths and patios) cost much more than plants and lawns, so don't get too carried away when considering them.

Next make a rough plan, marking in the boundary fences or walls, together with the outline of the house and any other fixed features. Then sketch in general

PLANNING TIPS

✔ If you've made a mistake and put a plant in the wrong spot, don't be afraid of moving it – plants of up to four or five years old can be moved successfully, especially in late autumn when they're dormant. While the soil is moist, dig a circle round the plant, then excavate as far as you can underneath it. Now lift it, retaining as much of the rootball as possible – some damage is inevitable, but very seldom fatal. Transfer it as quickly as possible to the new planting hole, fill in, firm down and water well. For the next year, keep the plant watered during any warm dry spells. Older plants are trickier, and can have enormous rootballs, but if your only option is to move them, then at least you're giving them a fighting chance of survival.

✔ When you view the garden from the house or from your favourite sitting-out spot, it's good to have a focal point where the eye can rest for a moment. A beautiful tree, a handsome pot or even a small statue, carefully sited, will really hold your garden picture together.

✔ Long narrow gardens are the trickiest of all to design. To avoid the 'tunnel' effect, break them up into a series of 'rooms' using plants, trellis, arches or pergolas. An area of lawn and trees, for instance, will look much more intriguing and inviting if it's first glimpsed through a rose-covered archway.

✔ If you're nervous about designing your garden, then it may pay you to get professional help. Be careful – there are lots of cowboys out there. Ask your friends if they can recommend anyone, or enquire at your local garden centre. When you find a likely designer, try to visit gardens they have worked on rather than looking at sketches and photographs. Alternatively, check through the gardening magazines – some of them run perfectly competent postal design services; this costs much less than hiring your own designer and though it's a bit impersonal, it will at least be a starting point.

✔ Gravel may seem like a good low maintenance idea, an inert covering for yards and yards of ground. But leaves litter in it in autumn and are fiddly to remove, soil infiltrates and weeds begin to sprout. So save it for smaller areas where, regularly raked or rolled, it will be an attractive feature without becoming a chore.

areas for borders, patio, paths, lawn and any other main features. Be logical: a meandering path through the lawn may look pretty, but no one will use it; sheds and compost heaps should, ideally, be placed where they'll be hidden from the house; a greenhouse must be in a sunny spot.

And that's really it for the first stage; it's not worth doing any more planning until you've done a bit of tidying up outside. This will give you the opportunity of getting to know your garden a bit better, and to mull over your initial thoughts.

THE HARD GRAFT

If you're pushed for time, concentrate your efforts on the back garden and leave the front until later. It's the back garden that you'll be relaxing in, so it deserves to be the priority.

If your garden is so neglected that you can't see the soil for the weeds, the simplest solution is to blast them with Tumbleweed or Round-up, so long as you avoid

This contemplative Buddha is a peaceful focal point in a lushly planted garden.

spraying any plants that you want to keep. They're highly effective weedkillers and leave no harmful residue in the soil, so that planting can begin as soon as the weeds have died and been cleared. If you're blessed with really persistent weeds such as bindweed or brambles, wait a month or so and give a second application to any re-growth.

In a brand new garden, the chances are that the builders have left it in quite a state, even if they've hidden it under a token sprinkling of topsoil. So the first job is to dig the garden over. Go down one fork's depth and prepare to be horrified by the amount of rubble, wood and old cement bags that you have to remove. This initial digging also helps to open up the soil, relieving any compaction caused by the builders' heavy machinery.

If the soil is poor, improve it by digging in as much organic matter as your purse and your patience will allow. All is explained in our 'Soil Care' chapter. It's hard work, but a wise investment – plants will flourish where otherwise they would either have sulked miserably or even have died.

While you're out there, lean on the fork from time to time, to note the hot spots and any that remain in shade

Mixing two materials such as brick and gravel makes a real impact and softens the look of a hard surfaced area.

all day – if your rough plan was right, the sitting out areas or patio are in the sunny spots. It's also worth checking whether any part of the garden is particularly windy, so that you can plan for plants to provide shelter.

The final factor to consider before making a more detailed plan is to look at what's beyond your boundary. Is there an ugly view that you might want to screen off? Or, if your luck's in, a lovely view that you certainly wouldn't want to hide when you plant the garden.

EVERGREEN ARCHITECTURE

Never underestimate the importance of evergreen plants in the garden. They provide its basic structure, making an excellent foil for other plants and flowers in summer and coming into their own in winter, giving shape to the garden when all else is lifeless and formless. Use them wisely – a spire-shaped conifer to mark an intersection, or two of them to flank a vista; sweetly scented choisya to

make a dome of glossy green where it can be seen from the kitchen window; a clipped holly trained on a single stem to make a wonderfully formal tree.

Evergreen hedges can be used to define the boundaries of the garden, or even to divide it up into compartments. But please, we beg, don't plant Leyland cypress. Yes, it gives you an almost instant screen, but after that you've the choice of

spending the rest of your lifetime trying to keep it down to size, or of having permanently disgruntled neighbours as it looms over their garden and deprives it of light and nutrients.

If you can afford it, plant a yew hedge and pamper it. With regular feeding and watering it can grow at a quite respectable rate, and its dense, dark green foliage always looks incomparably rich and classy.

MAKING THE FINAL PLAN

At this stage, real enthusiasts will prepare a scale plan on squared paper, using a thick dark pen to mark the site boundaries and any features that you want to retain (or have to retain – manhole covers, for instance, are somewhat permanent). Having made the base plan, stick a piece of tracing paper over it and mark in the proposed layout of patio, paths, lawn, borders and other major features such as trees. Try out several ideas on separate sheets of tracing paper, then spend time comparing them until you've reached a consensus with any other interested parties.

You can, of course, skip this stage and go straight on to the next, which is to mark out the whole plan on the ground. String and pegs can be used to mark out features like patios, hosepipe is ideal for showing the position of curved borders and lawns, and large bamboo canes can be stand-ins for trees. When you've finished all the 'left a bit, right a bit' business, take a look at the layout from an upstairs window, just to check whether it looks right from there as well.

SCREENING EYESORES

There are two types of eyesores you may want to screen – your own, and other people's.

In your own garden, you may want to hide the compost heap or an ugly shed. For the shed, you could simply grow an attractive climber on it, or in both instances, free-standing trellis planted with a climber would do the trick. Ugly walls, too, will benefit from a soft blanket of climbers. Even manhole covers can be disguised, by removing the cover and replacing it with one of the ingenious recessed planters that are available at larger garden centres.

Eyesores outside the garden are often most effectively screened by trees, and it's worth taking a little trouble to site them properly. Find an assistant who can safely handle a long pole (such as two 2.4m/8ft bamboo canes lashed together), then stand close to the house and direct the assistant, holding the pole upright, between you and the eyesore. You will eventually hit on just the right spot and it's surprising how small a tree can mask, or at least soften, the offending view.

This spendid pergola makes a highly decorative screen for that most mundane of all garden objects, the domestic dustbin.

GETTING GOING

Try to carry out the messiest work first. Generally this is the hard landscaping, building the patios and paths. Lay the paths first, so that you have a good surface to work from, and once the patio's built, you can at least have a sit down every so often.

If you don't want to tackle the soft landscaping (the plants) all in one go, lay the rest of the garden to lawn, and develop beds and borders as time and money allow. Mowing an extra bit of lawn is a lot less work than keeping empty borders looking tidy and weed-free. But do try to plant any trees as soon as possible – they'll give instant structure to the garden, and because they can take a couple of years to start growing away strongly, you'll be giving them a head start.

When you do develop the beds and borders, plant the shrubs first – they're the 'backbone' of the garden and it's much easier to decide where they should go if you haven't already confused the issue by putting in the herbaceous perennials. In the first few years, until your permanent plants fill out, there will inevitably be gaps, so plug them with colourful annuals or bedding plants in summer.

ASSESSING AN ESTABLISHED GARDEN

If you've moved to a house with an established garden, take at least a year to get to know it before making any changes. Some of the plants may be a bit of a mystery, but most decent garden centres should be happy to identify them if you take along a sample of leaves or flowers.

Aim simply to keep the garden under control during this period, cutting the lawn to keep it trim and healthy and keeping weeds at bay. Never be too hasty in condemning a plant. That dull shrub may next month produce a mass of exotic flowers. That tangled old apple tree could be properly pruned and become a beautiful and productive feature. Both would take years or even decades to replace. So give all plants a year's grace and if, after that, there are any that you truly dislike, then take them out.

These guidelines apply equally well to your own long-established garden, and an excellent way of 'previewing' changes is outlined in Graham Rice's superb book *The Complete Small Garden*. Basically, take a photograph from an upstairs window, enlarge it, then use sheets of clear acetate and wipe-off pens (from the art shop) to mark your proposed changes. By superimposing them over the photograph, you'll be able to see pretty clearly how they're going to affect the look of the garden.

Colour scheming is a good approach to planting your beds and borders. These shades of red, bronze and plum-purple combine for an excitingly hot colour scheme.

Growing from seeds and cuttings

There's something magical about growing your own plants from seeds and cuttings. Even for experienced gardeners, there's still a thrill as the seedlings start to emerge, and a great sense of pride when a cutting produces its first new leaves.

It also cuts the cost of gardening dramatically. Most packets of seed are absolute bargains, with the potential to produce lots of plants at just a few pence each and cuttings are even better, because they're free.

Follow the basic rules and you'll find it one of the most satisfying and rewarding aspects of gardening. Have a go - you've nothing to lose except, perhaps, your windowsills.

GROWING FROM SEED

Garden centres sell a good range of the more popular seeds, but for a wider selection, including the very best new varieties, send for one of the free seed catalogues that are advertised in gardening magazines.

Many plants can be sown outdoors, but others need extra warmth and protection in the early stages, and these should be started off indoors – your seed packet will always advise.

SOWING SEED IN THE GARDEN

This is the simplest method of sowing seed. Many of the pretty cottage garden plants such as annual cornflowers, larkspur and sweet peas, as well as hardy biennials (wallflowers, forget-me-nots) and most vegetables are grown this way.

Check the recommended sowing time on the seed packet, which will also tell you whether the variety likes a sunny or semi-shady spot. Armed with this information, choose your patch, remove any weeds and fork it over, digging in garden compost or well rotted manure to give it a bit of a boost. Firm the soil by treading it down, and rake it level.

To sow annuals, mark out a series of mini-furrows to the recommended depth and planting distance. Sow the

A well-prepared seed-bed, and regular watering in the early stages, are essential for successful germination.

seed in the rows – large seeds are easy to set at the correct spacing, but with smaller ones you'll just have to try to distribute them as evenly as possible. Mark the rows with sticks, label them and water well, using a watering can fitted with a rose.

The seedlings emerge in straight lines, which greatly simplifies weed identification, and although they look rather regimented at first, they'll eventually join together in one dense mass. Any overcrowded clumps should be thinned out by pulling up surplus plants (trying not to disturb those that remain).

Biennials can be treated in the same way, but as they won't flower in the first year, you might want to start them off in a spare piece of ground, transferring them to their flowering position in autumn.

Vegetables are normally sown in longer rows, which you can mark out with string stretched between two pegs. To grow well, they need a richer soil than annuals and biennials, so be sure to work in plenty of well rotted manure.

All seedlings should be kept well watered, free of weeds, and protected from slugs. If cats are a problem (they love the newly turned ground), deter them with netting or a forest of short sticks.

SOWING SEED INDOORS

Many of our most popular summer bedding plants, as well as houseplants and tender crops like tomatoes and peppers, need warmth to get them growing so should be started off indoors, usually in spring.

Seed can be sown in seed trays, but for the average garden, where just a few plants of each variety will be needed, start them off in 9cm/3½in pots. Fill the pot with moist multipurpose or seed compost and firm it down gently. (Never use garden soil which will become compacted and can harbour disease.) Sow the seeds thinly and cover them to the recommended depth with a further layer of compost. Very small dust-like seeds may not need to be covered at all. Water lightly using a watering can with a fine rose.

Label the pots and if you have a heated propagator, pop them straight in. If the central heating boiler or airing cupboard is your heat source, cover the pots with a piece of clear plastic or taut clingfilm, to retain moisture. Most seeds germinate quite happily in a steady temperature of 15-20°C/60-70°F. As soon as the seedlings emerge, place them on a light windowsill, removing any covering.

When the seedlings are large enough to handle

Seperate out congested seedlings as soon as they are large enough to handle and pot them on into a tray of fresh compost.

(usually when they've got a couple of pairs of leaves) pot them on into fresh compost in seedtrays, or in special trays divided into individual cells. Larger seedlings which will eventually become sizeable plants can be transferred to individual pots up to 9cm/3½in diameter.

To transplant them, knock the side of the pot to loosen the compost, then gently tip out the contents. Holding a seedling by one of its leaves, ease it away from the group, trying to keep the roots intact. Never handle the stems, which bruise or break very easily.

Using a pencil or dibber, make a hole in the compost and insert the seedling. Firm it into place with the pencil, so that the bottom leaves are just clear of the compost, then water them and return them to the windowsill. Keep them moist but not soggy and after six weeks, start to feed once a week with liquid fertiliser.

If the plants are destined for the garden it's best to toughen them up, because night-time conditions will be much cooler than they're used to. A couple of weeks beforehand, put them outside in a warm, sheltered spot during the day, bringing them in at night. In the second week, leave them outside all the time, but bring them in if frost is forecast.

GROWING FROM CUTTINGS

The terms for the different types of cuttings – softwood, semi-ripe and hardwood – look daunting on paper, but once you've had a good look at the plant that you want to propagate, they'll begin to make sense.

Softwood cuttings: This method, using soft new growth in spring or early summer, gives the quickest results, with cuttings rooting in one to eight weeks.

Using a sharp knife, take cuttings about 10cm/4in long from the tips of healthy shoots, putting them

---

SEED GROWING TIPS

✔ *To avoid seedlings becoming leggy on the windowsill, cover a piece of cardboard with silver foil and place it behind the seedlings. The foil reflects light from the window onto the plants, helping them grow much more sturdily.*

✔ *Very small seeds are easier to sow if mixed with fine sand, helping to produce a more even distribution of the seeds.*

✔ *Some seeds are more difficult to grow than others. Seed packets generally give an indication, but geraniums, lobelia, begonia, petunia, verbena and busy lizzies are among those best left to more experienced gardeners.*

✔ *Instead of covering pot-grown seeds with compost, you can use vermiculite. This lightweight material holds warmth and moisture, and improves germination rates.*

✔ *Many plants will root simply in water. So try snippings from your houseplants, and any garden plant that takes your fancy – ivies, willows and winter jasmine are especially easy.*

✔ *When taking clematis cuttings, use the softwood or semi-ripe methods, but always cut half-way between leaf joints, rather than just below. The smaller 'species' clematis root much more readily than the large-flowered hybrids.*

✔ *When chopping up a long stem for hardwood cuttings, make a slanting cut at the base of each portion and a straight cut at the top. That way, you'll be sure to put them in the right way up.*

✔ *Always remove flowers from cuttings – you need to keep their minds on the job in hand, rather than diverting their energy into flowering.*

straight into a polythene bag to prevent them from drying out. Fill a pot with multipurpose compost and firm it down gently.

Trim each cutting just below a leaf joint, reducing its length to about 7.5cm/3in. Strip the bottom 5cm/2in of leaves and dip the base of the cutting in hormone rooting powder. Insert the cutting in the compost to half its length, firming the soil around it. Once the pot is full (a 7.5cm/3in pot can take three or more cuttings), water well.

Softwood cuttings root most quickly in a heated propagator. The alternative is to cover each pot with a clear polythene bag, propping it with sticks so that it sits well clear of the leaves and securing it with an elastic

The use of hormone rooting powder encourages root production.

band. This can then be placed in a warm light spot, away from direct sunlight.

Check occasionally to see whether the pots need a little extra water. Once cuttings have rooted and are growing strongly, they can be separated and grown on in individual pots, uncovered, in a warm light place.

Plants to grow from softwood cuttings include geraniums, fuchsias and most houseplants. Garden plants such as forsythia, heathers, hydrangea, lavatera and potentilla, will also root well.

Semi-ripe cuttings: This is a good method for many garden shrubs and climbers, with cuttings taken any time from July to early autumn.

Sideshoots normally yield the best material for semi-ripe cuttings. You need those that are 10-15cm/4-6in long and are just beginning to become woody at the base, making your cut just below a leaf joint. Thereafter, semi-ripe cuttings can be treated in exactly the same way as softwood cuttings, though you don't need to keep them covered.

Good plants to grow from semi-ripe cuttings are ceanothus, choisya, holly, honeysuckle, lavender, mahonia, pyracantha, rose, viburnum and weigela.

Hardwood cuttings: This is the slowest method, but by far the simplest, requiring just a spare piece of ground and a little patience.

October and November are the best months for taking hardwood cuttings, and first you should prepare the ground by digging it over until the soil is open and crumbly. Next make a narrow V-shaped trench about 15cm/6in deep by inserting your spade and rocking it back and forth. Coarse sand (from the garden centre – never builder's sand) stimulates rooting, so place a 2.5cm/1in layer in the base.

Now choose strong young shoots (those that were produced this year), about the thickness of a pencil. Snip off 23cm/9in lengths, cutting just below a bud at the base and just above a bud at the top. Dip the base of each cutting in hormone rooting powder, then line them up in the trench 15cm/6in apart and firm the soil around them. Finally, label and water well. The rooted cuttings can be transplanted the following autumn.

Some of the more popular plants easily propagated by hardwood cuttings include buddleia, cotoneaster, forsythia, honeysuckle, jasmine, ivy, philadelphus (mock orange), ribes (flowering currant), roses and spiraea – but it's worth having a go with any woody plant.

Hanging baskets and window boxes

Put a hanging basket bursting with flowers by the front door or place a newly planted window box on a ledge and a most amazing thing happens. The whole area immediately brightens up, feels warmer and more welcoming. That's why some of the best and most inviting displays are seen outside pubs.

Although hanging baskets and window boxes are by no means an essential part of gardening, like all life's frivolities they're guaranteed to lift the heart and put a skip in the step.

They are, we admit, fiddly to look after – all that watering, feeding and dead-heading, but try to spare the time for just one or two. They'll keep you cheerful for months on end.

GROWING SUCCESS
HANGING BASKETS

Hanging baskets are available in a range of shapes and sizes, but the round wire basket is still the traditional favourite. These can be planted around the sides as well as the top, so that you can cram in a mass of plants for a really bold, lush display.

They need to be lined, of course, to retain the compost, and fresh green sphagnum moss blends in best with the plants, though there's also a synthetic moss substitute which looks almost like the real thing. Wool, fibre and rigid liners are also available, but they're not nearly so attractive – planting up is easier, but they're so ugly you'll probably regret ever having bought them.

Plastic baskets are undoubtedly easier to plant, because they don't need lining. Easier to care for too, since they don't dry out as quickly and some versions even have built in self watering devices. But somehow, even when in full flower, they never look quite as natural as the wire baskets.

WINDOW BOXES

Garden centres sell a wide range of window boxes in terracotta, wood or plastic. Their relative merits are discussed in 'Container Gardening' (see page 29) but there are some specific points worth considering, whichever you choose.

Larger, deeper boxes hold more compost and need less frequent watering. However, a large box placed in front of a small window can block lots of daylight, so you'll probably have to compromise. One of the best solutions is to position and support the box just below the window ledge, allowing plenty of room for growth, especially if you have side-opening windows.

All shades of pink, from the palest to deep rose, make a wonderfully harmonious window box planting.

PLANTING AND CARING FOR A SUMMER BASKET

Planting up a wire basket is labour-intensive, but not difficult, and the layered planting produces the most spectacular results.

● Sit the basket on a bucket to keep it steady during planting. Line the bottom with a 2.5cm/1in layer of moss and place a plastic saucer on it to act as a reservoir when watering.

● Use bush lobelia or something similar as your 'base' plant to form a full globe of background colour, setting it 7.5cm/3in apart in a circle. Work from the inside, carefully pushing the leaves through the gaps in the basket and resting the roots on the moss.

● Add another layer of moss round the side of the basket, to the half-way mark. Plant a second circle of lobelia, positioning it so that it doesn't overhang the plants of the first circle. Using hanging basket or multipurpose compost, fill in around the rootballs of the plants.

● Make a third layer of moss and plants, top up with compost, then moss the basket to the rim.

● Next plant the top of the basket, positioning the tallest upright plant (such as a geranium) in the centre, smaller upright plants around it, and trailing plants at the edges. (Don't worry about cramming lots in – the best baskets have plenty of plants, to provide a good show from the start.)

● Fill in any gaps with compost, water thoroughly and finally hang the basket in position on a strong well-secured bracket.

● From then onwards, the key to a long-lasting display is regular watering, feeding and dead-heading.

Watering is the most time-consuming chore once the weather warms up and plants are growing vigorously. So check the basket every day, and try to water in the early morning or in the cool of the evening. To avoid the effort of lifting a heavy watering can, use a 1 litre plastic bottle, which contains just about the right amount of water. Even easier, invest in a long hose-end lance .

Feeding won't be necessary for the first six weeks, but thereafter, feed once a week with a high potash fertiliser such as liquid tomato food.

Dead-heading, the regular removal of faded blooms, not only keeps the basket looking good, it prevents the plants from going to seed and fading away.

PLANTING A WINDOW BOX

Planting up a window box is just like planting up any other container. It's essential to have drainage holes in the bottom, so make some if necessary. Add 5cm/2in of drainage material such as broken terracotta, then fill with multipurpose compost. Plant taller growing varieties at the back, then smaller and trailing plants at the front and sides. Firm down the compost, adding more if needed, water well and make sure the box is secure – you don't want it falling off in a gust of wind. Prolong the life of a wooden window box by planting up in a slightly smaller plastic trough.

Aftercare is the same as for hanging baskets, though it's unlikely you'll have to water every day, but do check regularly in hot, dry weather.

Making the most of Summer Colour

Most people mix lots of different plants and flower colours in the same basket or box, and it can look lovely. But you'll get some even better effects if you're slightly more selective. Experiment with simple colour schemes – warm colours like gold, orange and red look great together, as do cool blues and whites. Or go for a blend of similar colours, for instance white, pale pink and rose pink. If you're feeling more adventurous, the most striking schemes are based on really strong contrasts like yellow with purple, blue with orange and red with green.

FLOWERING PLANTS

Flowering plants are the obvious first choice for boxes and baskets, but there are some very pretty foliage plants which will add an extra splash of colour. Look out, in particular, for varieties with bronze, gold, or white-variegated leaves. And silver leaved plants like *Lotus berthelotii* and helichrysum blend beautifully with pink, white or blue flowers.

It's always difficult to judge which plants will look good together, but one of the easiest ways is to wander round the garden centre, gathering up all the plants you think you might like and putting them in a window box or basket which is roughly the same size as the one you've got at home. If one plant or colour doesn't fit your scheme, then swap it over until you've got the perfect combination.

Of course, you don't have to confine yourself to bedding plants – it's great fun to experiment with

The rich, hot colours of geraniums and verbena, teamed with dark blue lobelia, make a tremendous impact.

other groups of plants. One of the prettiest baskets we've ever seen was crammed full of colourful herbs, a happy riot of golden marjoram, silver thyme, purple sage, daisy-flowered chamomile and a few bright nasturtiums with their peppery-flavoured leaves.

Window boxes offer even more scope for greedy gardeners, and can be used for raising vegetables like young carrots, dwarf beans, radishes, spring onions, baby beet, rocket, chili peppers and frilly red-leaved lettuces. Placed on a kitchen windowsill, there's nothing to beat them for fast food.

Making the most of

Winter Colour

At the end of summer, your plants will be giving up the ghost (and who can blame them, they must be exhausted). But don't just empty the basket and leave it in the shed to hibernate – give it a new lease of life.

From September onwards, garden centres sell a range of small evergreens such as miniature conifers which are ideal as replacements for the taller bedding plants in the centre of the basket. Around these, plant colourful heathers, wonderful winter flowering pansies, and to give it some real oomph for spring, don't forget to pop in some dwarf bulbs. As a finishing touch, plant variegated trailing ivy round the edges.

The basket will look lovely from autumn through to late spring and (cheering, this) you'll find it needs far less care than the summer basket. There's no need to feed it – just give it an occasional watering if it's necessary over winter, and water more regularly in spring as the weather warms up.

Don't give up on your window boxes either. One of the simplest schemes is a mass of winter flowering pansies (it's particularly effective if they're all the same colour) underplanted with bulbs such as dwarf narcissi or rockery tulips. To add height and extra interest you could also put in some of the small evergreens – golden leaved forms are especially good since they will look bright and cheerful even in the depths of winter.

In this wall basket lined with old fern fronds, hellebores are planted with snowdrops and cyclamen to bring colour and cheer in late winter.

SITING AND SECURITY

A hanging basket, fully planted and well watered, can be very heavy so it's important that the bracket is strong enough to take the weight and is securely fixed to the wall.

Depending on your choice of plants, baskets can be hung in most positions, but they're never very successful in windy spots. Most will withstand the occasional buffeting, but not constant wear and tear. Sheltered positions really are the best.

Window boxes, too, can be extremely heavy and must be fixed securely in place. On sills that slope forwards, put small wedges at the front of the box to keep it level, and fix metal brackets to the sides of the window recess or to the sill itself to prevent the box from slipping forwards.

It's well worth placing a plastic tray under the window box to stop excess water from running down the side of the building. And if you're a high-rise gardener it'll stop your neighbours getting dripped on.

Top Ten Plants for Hanging Baskets and Window Boxes

Tuberous–rooted begonias

❀ BEGONIAS

The fibrous rooted semperflorens varieties are superb, with a neat, rounded habit, glossy green or dark bronze foliage and red, white or pink flowers all summer. Tuberous rooted begonias are much larger (to 60cm/2ft) and more flamboyant with large double flowers in startlingly electric colours; in our opinion, the upright varieties are much better than the trailing forms. All begonias will grow in sun or shade.

❀ BIDENS

A wonderfully vigorous trailing plant with ferny leaves and masses of starry gold flowers through summer. It can become slightly untidy and may need occasional trimming to keep it under control. One of its many virtues is that it's remarkably tough and can happily withstand being dried out for a few days – once watered it will start

Brachycome with fried egg plant

growing again as if nothing had happened. Best in a sunny spot.

❀ BRACHYCOME
(Swan river daisy)

This bushy 25cm/10in plant is a real gem in a sunny, sheltered spot, making mounds of finely cut leaves studded with tiny daisy flowers. The best of the colours is the pale purple, almost blue, shade – the pinks and whites can look rather washed out. Apart from being extremely pretty, the flowers are invaluable in hanging baskets because they close up when thirsty; a useful reminder to get the watering can out.

Bidens with trailing helichrysum

PLANTING TIPS

✔ *Baskets and boxes can be successful in light shade, but you need to be more careful in the plants you choose. Busy lizzies, begonias, fuchsias, tobacco plants and variegated ivies are particularly good.*

✔ *It's impossible to water a hanging basket that has completely dried out; instead sit it in a deep bowl of water for a couple of hours and let it have a really good soak.*

✔ *To preserve your (expensive) wooden window boxes, use a plastic box as a liner so that soil does not come into contact with the wood and encourage rotting.*

✔ *Don't forget that summer baskets and boxes should never be placed outdoors until all danger of frost has passed. If you want to get a head-start on the neighbours, plant them up early and grow them on in a light, frost-free spot.*

❀ BUSY LIZZIE (Impatiens)

Among the finest and most versatile of all bedding plants, busy lizzies put on a wonderful display whatever the weather, flower from June to the first frosts, and are available in a wide range of colours. Look out for the 'Super Elfin' series which are more compact and therefore better suited to baskets and boxes. Good in sun or shade, they can also tolerate a bit of neglect.

❀ GERANIUM (Pelargonium)

The perennial classic for sunny positions, looking superb all summer. Use the upright varieties in the centre of the basket or back of the window box and plant trailing

Busy lizzie (Impatiens)

forms at the edge. Just for a change from the mop-head types, try the continental 'balcony' trailers in window boxes – airy sprays of flowers on vigorous plants. Geraniums are remarkably tough and soon bounce back if you forget to water them.

❀ HELICHRYSUM PETIOLARE

Spreading, trailing foliage plants that add invaluable structure as well as attractive leaf colour to planting schemes. The soft felted leaves come in a variety of colours and the silvery grey is the best known (the small-leaved compact form is especially good). Yellow and variegated helichrysums are also excellent. Best in sunny positions, they are very drought tolerant.

❀ PANSY

Winter and spring flowering pansies are by far the best; don't bother with the summer varieties which suffer very badly if you forget to water them. Available in a superb range of colours, nothing can beat them in spring displays. Among the most charming are the tiny 'Princess' violas, best grown in boxes and baskets close to the house where you can enjoy their cheerful faces in glorious close-up.

Balcony geraniums

Pansies

Petunias

❀ PETUNIA

Best in sunny positions, petunias will provide a fine display in all but the wettest summers. The 'Surfinia' type is particularly splendid, but incredibly vigorous. Three plants will fill a 35cm/14in basket on their own, and trail as much as 1.2m/4ft, bushing out almost as wide. The new compact 'Junior' types are much less domineering, however. All petunias need to be dead-headed regularly to ensure continuity of flower.

❀ SMALL EVERGREENS

Available in garden centres in autumn, these are invaluable for winter and spring displays. Dwarf or slow growing conifers, golden leaved *Euonymus fortunei* 'Emerald 'n' Gold' or white variegated 'Silver Queen', and small skimmias make good centrepieces and can be planted in the garden when containers are needed for summer bedding. Winter flowering or colourful foliage heathers provide an excellent contrast in

the foreground, and small variegated ivies can be planted at the front.

❀ VERBENA

Mainly available in trailing form, spicily scented verbenas flower from early summer until the first frosts – lovely plants that really earn their keep, with a continuous succession of pincushion clusters of flower. Some can be prone to mildew, but amongst the resistant strains are soft pink 'Silver Anne', cerise pink 'Sissinghurst' and scarlet 'Lawrence Johnston'.

Verbena 'Amethyst'

Hardy perennials

'Hardy perennial' is a handy catch-all term for a huge range of plants, but basically it means any long-lived frostproof plant that isn't a tree, shrub or climber.

Stately delphiniums: the essence of an English summer garden.

The major group is the flowering herbaceous perennials – those wonderful plants that fill our spring and summer borders with colour and die back to the ground in winter – and there are yet others, like grasses and ferns, that we grow for the beauty of their foliage.

Long-lived, trouble-free, increasing in beauty year by year, they'll give you enormous pleasure in return for very little effort.

GROWING SUCCESS

Most hardy perennials will be with you for a very long time, so it's worth giving them a hearty welcome by preparing the ground well before planting. Fork it over to open it up and mix in plenty of organic matter such as compost or well-rotted horse manure.

Water your plants and set them in the ground at the same level as they were in the pot, firming the soil around them. Water again, and keep watered for the first few weeks if the weather is dry. They don't need any regular feeding, but a spring boost of fish, blood and bone (smells awful, works wonders as long as you keep the dog off it) and a mulch of organic matter will be gratefully received.

Exploit the wonderful diversity of hosta leaf shapes, colour and forms.

Flowering plants can be kept looking neat by removing faded flowerheads, and they'll often reward you with a second, smaller flush of blooms. Most perennials die back in winter and the old growth can be

LEAFY PERENNIALS

Although we tend to think of hardy perennials in terms of flowery summer borders, there are some that have a lot to offer in the beauty of their foliage. The large sculpted leaves of **hostas** make them an obvious first choice, but there are other plants which are easy to overlook at first glance but will become firm favourites.

Pulmonaria (lungwort), despite the name, is a pretty little thing. After the spring display of blue, white or red flowers, the leaves take over, forming dense silver-splashed rosettes which look their best in a shady spot in damp soil.

For the front of a sunny border, try low-growing **lamb's ears** *(Stachys lanata/byzantina)*; the silvery leaves are thickly felted and the temptation to stroke them is irresistible. The tall spikes of purple flower are a bonus.

Investigate the **grasses**, too. Most of the fine-leaved festucas are an intense silver-blue, especially in a sunny spot, and grow into mounded hummocks which look like sleeping hedgehogs. And there's a lovely golden grass worth tracking down, *Milium effusum* 'Aureum' (Bowles' golden grass); in a moist soil it makes an arching fountain of soft leaves which will light up a shady spot, and it seeds itself about obligingly .

Finally, **ferns**, which seem to be creeping back into fashion. Though normally associated with moist conditions, many will thrive in drier soil, so always check the growing instructions. The prettiest of the smaller types is the soft shield fern *(Polystichum setiferum)*, with lacy fronds of fresh green.

And if it's a giant you want, try *Osmunda regalis*, the royal fern, which can reach 1.3m/5ft in captivity.

A combination of contrasting leaf sizes, forms and textures makes a long-lasting display.

cut down to ground level in late autumn.

DIVISION

Many hardy perennials will spread into quite substantial clumps, and after three or four years the centre of the clump can become overcrowded and produce fewer flowers. So to rejuvenate them, and increase your stocks, divide them up.

The best time to do this is in October (when they'll be starting to go dormant) or March (when they'll be eager to get growing). Water the plants if the soil is dry, then dig round them with a fork and lift the whole clump, taking as much root as possible.

This is where the fun begins, because while some will separate into plantlets simply by teasing them apart, others are so woody that you may have to resort to chopping through them with the spade or a sharp knife. It sounds brutal, but so long as each portion has a reasonable number of roots attached, it should come to no harm. Picking out the best, most vigorous plantlets, replant at the original depth, and start all over again.

But just a word of warning: some perennials are poisonous or have irritant sap, so if in doubt, always wear gloves.

Two forks back to back can be used to prise clumps apart.

The resulting smaller clumps can usually be divided by hand.

Replant in well-prepared soil and water thoroughly.

Making the most of Peonies

Peonies are by far the most glamorous of all hardy perennials, with great luscious heads of single or ruffled double flowers in all shades from deepest red to pure white. Their season's all too short – just a few weeks in May or June – but we do urge you to grow them; you'll carry the memory of those sumptuous flowers right through the year.

Paeonia lactiflora
'Bowl of Beauty'

But, like all great beauties, they should be cherished and given all those extra little attentions that will keep them at their loveliest.

They must have a sunny well drained spot, liberally enriched with organic matter, and it's vital that you plant them at the right depth – too deep and they'll refuse to flower. The crown (the point from which top growth starts) should be no more than 2.5cm/1in below ground level.

The flowers of the double varieties are so full and heavy that they can bend right to the ground unless you support them. 'Grow through' plant supports are ideal, allowing each flower stem to be individually spaced, but you could compromise with a dense network of twiggy sticks.

When it comes to the spring mulch, keep it at a respectful distance by placing it around rather than over the plants. These are fastidious creatures and object strongly to dollops of manure on their heads.

Finally, put up a 'do not disturb' sign; they hate to be moved. If you're forced to do so, expect a temper tantrum and no flowers for several years.

Peonies are amazingly long-lived. They can last for 50 years and more, and if you treat them with the respect they deserve, they'll never look a day over 25.

LONG-LASTING COLOUR

The bold colours of ruby penstemon and purple salvia are toned down by a soft pink rose.

Hardy perennials give you terrific scope for playing around with colour. If you want to be really bold, plant a whole group of the 'hot' colours – red-orange kniphofia (red-hot poker), scarlet oriental poppies, ruby-flowered sedums, flaming orange crocosmia (montbretia), golden achillea (yarrow) and rudbeckia (black-eyed Susan), gaily striped gaillardias, rich orange, red or yellow helianthemums and crimson penstemons. It sounds horribly gaudy, but if you tone it down with a few foliage plants, you can achieve some wonderful effects.

Those of a nervous disposition might like to try a quieter scheme in the tried and tested formula of pink, white and blue. Nepeta (catmint) gives a long-lasting haze of soft blue, as does the lower-growing scabious 'Butterfly Blue'. Pink can be provided by hardy geraniums, peonies, astilbes and (appropriately enough) the garden pinks – those sweetly clove-scented varieties of dianthus. For white, a mist of tall gypsophila, groups of Shasta daisies, white forms of *Anemone japonica*, white campanulas and the best of the white asters, 'Monte Casino'. Delphiniums, of course, come conveniently in all three colours.

Top Ten Hardy Perennials

❀ ALCHEMILLA MOLLIS (Lady's mantle)

A real charmer – soft green scalloped leaves and airy plumes of acid-yellow flowers in June/July, to 45cm/18in. They seed freely and will establish in all sorts of nooks and crannies. Cut them back almost to ground level in early August for a fresh show of tender young leaves

PLANTING TIPS

✔ *Hardy perennials always look best planted in groups of three or five. An expensive operation, but you could always buy one plant and divide it up after a couple of years. And look out for the larger plants at garden centres – very often they're so mature that they can be split up before planting.*

✔ *The lush spring growth of many hardy perennials is manna from heaven for slugs. So protect those you know are vulnerable – delphiniums, in particular, can be stripped overnight.*

✔ *If you've got a damp spot in the garden, there are a number of hardy perennials that will thrive, including hemerocallis (day lily), filipendula, Primula japonica, mimulus, monarda (bergamot), rodgersia, lythrum (purple loosestrife) and astilbes.*

✔ *Some of the most unearthly colours in the whole of gardening are to be found amongst the prickly eryngiums (sea hollies). Steely silvers and blue-purples, with a metallic sheen to leaves and flowers. They make excellent dried flowers or can be left uncut through winter as dramatically architectural skeletons.*

and (with luck) a sprinkling of flowers. Alchemilla is completely pest and disease free and grows anywhere and everywhere, but is especially good as a softening edge for paths and patios.

❀ CAMPANULA (Bellflower)

Campanulas are one of the easiest cottage garden flowers, needing only well-drained soil, in sun or partial shade. The lowest-growing, *C. carpatica*, is lovely for the front of the border, with wide upturned blue or white flowers in July and August. If you've a yen for harebells, choose *C. persicifolia* – tall spikes of delicate white or blue flower to 90cm/3ft on wiry stems, from June to August. And most striking of all, *C. lactiflora*, with huge heads of milky-blue bells to 1.2m/4ft in June and July. Any, and every, campanula is worth growing.

❀ CROCOSMIA (Montbretia)

One of the joys of late summer, with arching stems of blazing orange-red flowers above spearlike leaves. One of the most outstanding is 'Lucifer', the flame-orange flowers topping 90cm/3ft, and of the slightly shorter

Euphorbia polychroma

varieties, 'Firebird' and burnt-orange 'Emberglow' are excellent. Plants eventually form dense stands, which can be lifted and divided with a sharp spade. Give crocosmias a sunny position in well-drained soil. Pest and disease free, these are easy, showy plants for anyone to grow.

❀ DELPHINIUM

Classic midsummer flowers, soaring to 1.8m/6ft – demanding plants, but breathtaking when well grown. Give them a rich soil in a sunny sheltered spot, and in spring protect the emerging shoots and young foliage from slugs. To keep them on the straight and narrow, provide stout canes for the flowers from an early stage, tying them in as they grow. Cut out the flower spikes as soon as they fade to encourage a second, smaller crop. Be extra generous when mulching in spring. Just a note: Pacific Hybrid/Giant delphiniums are very short-lived, so stick to named English varieties such as dark blue 'Fenella'.

❀ EUPHORBIA

Euphorbias are remarkably varied and the most striking is *E. wulfenii*, with bottle-brush stems of grey-green leaves topped by cylindrical heads of long-lasting sulphur-yellow flower bracts in spring, to 90cm/3ft. By contrast, *E. polychroma* is a neatly domed plant, to 45cm/18in, with bright yellow bracts. Most euphorbias do best in sun, on any ordinary soil, but for ground cover for impossible places use *E. robbiae*, with handsome dark green leaves; it happily spreads in even the driest shade. Take care when cutting out flowered stems – the sap is a severe irritant.

Geranium *'Johnson's Blue'*

❀ GERANIUM

Good tempered, undemanding, pest and disease free, excellent groundcover, neatly domed shape, and smothered in a succession of delightful small flowers, hardy garden geraniums will grow anywhere, for anyone. Colours range from white, through all the pinks to violet and deepest purple. For dry shade, opt for pink *G. macrorrhizum* and for general garden use look out for 'A.T. Johnson', an exceptionally long-flowering silver-pink and 'Buxton's Variety' a saucer-shaped sky blue with a white centre. Cut hard back after flowering – there's often a repeat performance.

❀ HELLEBORUS

For winter and early spring flower, hellebores are a must. The true Christmas rose, *Helleborus niger*, can be tricky, but the less demanding *H. orientalis* hybrids, flowering in early spring, are equally lovely and have a good colour range from white to deepest plum. To show off the low-growing flowers, cut out the older leaves and surround the plant with a layer of bark chips to prevent soil-splashes. Hellebores enjoy partial shade and a fertile, moisture-retentive (but not waterlogged) soil.

❀ HOSTA

Hostas are the most architectural of all herbaceous plants, forming wide rosettes of sculpted leaves. *H. sieboldiana elegans* is the noblest of them all – enormous blue-grey leaves up to 30cm/1ft across and deeply ribbed. The *H. fortunei* varieties are rather smaller with some excellent variegated forms. Hostas can (and should) be used almost anywhere in the garden – the soil must be reasonably fertile, but they'll grow in sun or partial shade, and the only situation they really dislike is a hot dry spot. But they do need protection from slugs or they'll be sadly tattered by midsummer.

❀ PAEONIA (Peony)

Peonies appear in May and June and, roses apart, there's nothing that can match them at that time of year. They're often sold simply as 'red', 'white' and so on, but if you get the chance to pick out named varieties, look for the sumptuous doubles. 'Duchesse de Nemours' is a ruffled globe of white, 'Felix Crousse' a rich crimson red, 'Sarah Bernhardt'

Hellebore flowers

apple blossom pink, and all deliciously scented. Peonies grow to around 90cm/3ft, and the leaves remain an attractive feature throughout summer. Once established they'll live for many years, and if you follow our guidelines in 'Making the most of Peonies' you won't go far wrong.

❀ PHLOX PANICULATA

One of the old faithfuls of the flower border, making increasingly wide stands of 90cm/3ft stems, topped with clusters of flowers from July to September. It's a tough, undemanding plant in sun or partial shade and a fertile soil. On soils which tend to dry out, you'll find that it droops and will need extra watering. The colours are wonderful, from pure white to scarlet, mauve and cerise. One of the prettiest is 'Sandringham', a cyclamen pink with a deeper pink eye. To increase your stocks, just lift and divide them in October, replanting the best portions.

IDEAS FOR LOW-MAINTENANCE

✔ *Many hardy perennials make excellent ground cover plants, either by virtue of their dense ground-hugging leaf cover or because they make an impenetrable mat of roots close to the surface. Alchemilla, ajuga (bugle), hostas and geraniums are all particularly good.*

✔ *Lysimachia (creeping Jenny) is an instant charmer with its buttercup flowers, but it's somewhat invasive and may have to be cleared back. So avoid planting it on heavy soils where the underground stems and tenacious roots will be almost impossible to remove completely.*

Standard bay trees flank a collection of
herbs grown in pots.

Herbs

Herbs are such virtuous plants. Easy to please, pest and disease free, decorative, aromatic, magnets for bees and butterflies. And most important of all, delicious – freshly picked herbs can transform a dish from the mediocre to the sublime. A little tarragon inside the chicken as it roasts, a sprig of rosemary with the lamb, a sprinkle of basil on sliced tomatoes; happy eating guaranteed.

So throw away those little jars of tired dried leaves, tasting of tired dried leaves, and invest in the real thing – a living plant full of freshness and flavour.

GROWING SUCCESS

Almost without exception, herbs are ridiculously easy to grow. Starting from seed is the cheapest option, and specialist seedsmen like Suffolk Herbs have an astonishing range, but if you want an instant plant, garden centres are becoming much more adventurous and you should find a good selection.

Full sun and a well-drained soil suits most herbs best, but a few (parsley, mint, chervil, lovage and sorrel) can be grown in partial shade and moist (but not soggy) soil. There's generally no need to enrich the soil before planting, since herbs are not greedy plants, but do fork it over to improve the drainage. Heavy clay soils can be opened up by digging in plenty of gravel and organic matter such as compost or well-rotted manure. In pots, use a gritty compost like John Innes No. 2.

Set your plants in at the same level as they were in the pot, and water well. Keep them watered for the first few weeks if the weather is dry, but thereafter they need very little attention. Some varieties die down in winter, and the old leaves and stems can be cut back to ground level.

Most herbs are perfectly hardy and will live for many years, though a handful (such as chervil, coriander and dill) are annuals which grow, flower and die in one season, and will need to be replaced each spring. Parsley, too, is best grown fresh each year. The only really frost-sensitive herb that you're likely to meet is basil.

HERB PLANTINGS

A herb garden is a wonderful place – soft colours, rich scents, and the drone of contented bees. Playing around with foliage contrasts is great fun – spires of rosemary; spiky clumps of chives; smoky wisps of fennel, chervil and dill; dense mats of thyme; blocks of bright green parsley; a ferny haze of sweet cicely. One of the best ways of displaying herbs is to plant them in patterns, between the spokes of an old cartwheel, for instance – though only the neater, less rampant herbs should be used in such a confined space. The ultimate is to divide them into small beds edged with weathered brick; bricks and herbs make a magical harmony.

That's the ideal, of course, but if you can't spare the space for a whole herb plot, plant them in beds and borders. Grow thyme close to paths where you'll brush past and release the scent. Edge a formal border with a marching line of chives. Plant fennel as a filmy foil for roses.

In tiny gardens, grow herbs in pots in a sunny spot. Terracotta pots, though more expensive than plastic, always look good with herbs, and you can cluster them together to make a herb garden in miniature.

To harvest herbs, gather on a warm dry day, preferably before they are in full flower and hang them upside down in small bunches in a warm place – an airing cupboard is ideal. Once they're thoroughly brittle, crumble them up and pot them into jars. Dark glass jars are best or keep clear jars in a cupboard to exclude light.

Top Ten Essential Herbs

❀ BASIL

Basil is a pernickety herb, but so delicious that it's worth the extra care. A tender annual, it sulks if it's cold, so give it a sunny sheltered spot. It is best grown in pots in the greenhouse, where the powerful aroma from the leaves will banish whitefly, or on a bright windowsill indoors. As well as the plain green forms of basil, look out for the attractive purple and fancy-leaved varieties. Pinch out the growing tips to keep plants bushy, and remove any flowers.

❀ CHIVES

These reed-leaved members of the onion family are a cinch, cheerfully growing for even the most neglectful gardener. All they ask is ordinary garden soil, in sun or partial shade. Two close relatives are the Egyptian and Welsh onions – harder to find,

Chives

but equally tough. The leaves are fat and tubular, the flavour stronger, and the Egyptian has the extraordinary habit of producing tiny onion bulbs from its flowerheads.

❀ FENNEL

Aniseed-flavoured fennel is a beautiful herb with great plumes of feathery foliage to a height of 1.2m/4ft. Any soil will suit it, in full sun. In addition to their culinary virtues, the filigree leaves are extremely pretty in flower arrangements, especially if you grow the smoky purple form. Its close relation, Florence fennel, is an annual vegetable, valued for the highly flavoured 'bulb' at the base.

❀ MARJORAM

Marjoram, also known as oregano, has a nicely rounded flavour; rather like thyme, but smoother. Sweet or pot marjoram (*Origanum majorana*) should be grown as an annual, so for perennial pleasure you'll need wild marjoram (*Origanum vulgare*). This

makes spreading hummocks of soft small leaves, and the golden form, 'Aureum' really lights up the garden. Marjoram needs sun and a well-drained soil, plus an annual haircut after flowering.

❀ MINT

Mint has a uniquely clean, refreshing flavour, and the manners of a thug, spreading from runners and overwhelming anything in its path. So keep it caged. Growing it in pots is an ideal solution, but in the garden you can plant it in bottomless buckets

Chives

Silver-variegated thyme

Oregano

PLANTING TIPS

✔ *For a winter supply of fresh herbs like chives, parsley, mint, tarragon or thyme, pot them up in early August, cut them back and bring them indoors before the first frosts. Placed on a light window sill, they'll keep on cropping for months on end.*

✔ *Bay trees will grow happily in pots, and look very handsome flanking a doorway. Have a go at training yours into a pyramid, trimming the tree to shape while it's growing strongly in summer. In colder districts, and in severe weather, protect bays from frost damage by draping them with horticultural fleece.*

sunk into the ground. Mint prefers a moist soil, in sun or partial shade. Apple mint and spearmint have the finest flavour, but do look out for decorative variegated forms such as the gold-veined gingermint.

❀ PARSLEY

Though it's always available in pots, parsley is a more-ish herb, so if you want a good supply, grow it from seed. Forget all the myths about sowing the seeds naked at midnight, and so on; to germinate, and flourish, parsley must have a moist, fertile soil in sun or partial shade. So add plenty of organic matter before sowing, and keep the seedbed well watered until the seed has germinated. Technically, parsley is a biennial, but it's never as good in the

second year, so make fresh sowings each spring. Flat-leaved French parsley has by far the best flavour.

❀ ROSEMARY

With its spiky leaves, soft blue flowers and aromatic scent, rosemary is a valuable evergreen shrub in its own right, though not reliably hardy in colder areas. It needs well-drained soil and a sunny, sheltered position. As well as the more usual forms, look out for the tall, vigorous 'Miss Jessop's Upright' and the lovely arching 'Severn Sea'. To keep plants neat and bushy, cut all growths back by half in March each year.

❀ SAGE

In addition to its culinary merits, sage is another useful garden shrub – evergreen, hardy and a neatly domed shape. As well as the usual grey-green, there are gold-patterned and purple leaved forms which are excellent plants for a mixed border, and equally tasty. 'Tricolor', splashed with pink and white, is especially attractive but not so hardy as the rest. Give sage a sunny, well-drained soil, and cut back any straggly branches in spring to keep it bushy.

❀ TARRAGON

The tarragon that you grow from seed is Russian, and not nearly so good as French tarragon, which can only be bought as plants. If you know someone who grows it, beg a few of the runners that form around the

Marjoram

Sage

Parsley

Gold-variegated thyme

IDEAS FOR LOW-MAINTENANCE

✔ *Herbs, by their very nature, are low maintenance plants – they're virtually immune to pests and diseases and positively dislike being overwatered or overfed.*

✔ *Thyme, marjoram and sage, with their dense, spreading habit, are invaluable ground cover plants, smothering out all but the most persistent weeds. Lemon balm will do the same job, but seeds itself freely, so snip off the flowers – they're pretty insignificant anyway.*

✔ *For an aromatic informal hedge, use rosemary, planted at 90cm/3ft intervals. In warmer districts, the pretty blue flowers are produced almost continuously, and plants need only be trimmed once a year, in spring, to prevent them from becoming too straggly.*

plant, to grow on in your own garden. Does best on light soils, in sun. In colder districts, mound earth over plants in winter for frost protection.

❀ THYME

Of all the herbs, thyme is the most valued as a garden plant. Low spreading mounds of tiny leaves, in green, gold and silver-variegated forms, covered in bees at flowering time. Lovely in pots, as an edging, or to grow in walls and paving cracks. Thyme loves sun, and any ordinary well-drained soil. If plants become woody, chop them back by half in spring. The best for cooking are common thyme *(Thymus vulgaris)* and lemon thyme *(Thymus citriodorus)*.

Houseplants

Some people seem to have the happy knack of growing houseplants well, but if you're struggling, the trick is to think of them as the plant equivalent of zoo animals – captive creatures, far from home, doing their best to survive in an alien environment. Your job is to try to mimic their natural growing conditions; the right light, heat, watering and feeding – all the little home comforts.

A yucca grown with creeping fig (Ficus pumila) *and bird's nest fern* (Asplenium).

Some houseplants will inevitably cause problems – gardenias, for instance, are virtually impossible to grow well, but all the plants featured here should thrive for you.

GROWING SUCCESS
HOW TO CHOOSE
Buy plants at the peak of perfection. Look for buoyant leaves, healthy new shoots, sturdy growth and, on flowering plants, plenty of unopened buds. Reject any with yellowed or diseased leaves, spindly growth and, most important of all, any that have been allowed to dry out completely. And if the weather's cold, insist that the plant is well wrapped for the journey home, to keep it at an even temperature.

POSITION
Houseplant labels now carry much more information than they used to, so always check the recommended position. In general, few plants (cacti apart) will be happy in the full blaze of afternoon sun – most much prefer a spot on, or close to, a north, west or east facing window. In shady corners, try aspidistra, fatsia, ferns, kangaroo vine *(Cissus),* grape ivy *(Rhoicissus)* and marantas or calatheas, but keep an eye on them and move them into a lighter position if they're not growing well. All houseplants grow towards the nearest light source, so turning them now and again will prevent them from becoming lopsided.

TEMPERATURE
Most houseplants are perfectly content at normal room temperature and don't object to you turning off the heating at night, but in very cold weather don't leave plants trapped in the chilly gap between closed curtains and window glass. Some dislike the dry atmosphere of central heating and will let you know by developing crispy brown tips and margins to the leaves. If this happens, you should either mist them regularly (tricky, with furniture about) or stand them on saucers filled with pebbles or gravel. Keep the saucers topped up with water to just below the bottom of the pot, so that as the water evaporates they'll have their own moist microclimate.

For unheated bedrooms or porches, flowering houseplants such as cyclamen and chrysanthemums are ideal – they'll relish the conditions and flower for a much longer period. Ivies and aspidistras will also thrive here.

WATERING AND FEEDING
The frequency of watering depends on several factors – the plant, the position, the size of the pot, and the time of year, so there are no hard and fast rules. What you need to achieve is a balance; plants will object if they're kept dry for too long, but they'll equally turn up their noses (and often their toes) if they're given soggy conditions. It sounds tricky, but if you apply a bit of common sense you'll soon get the knack.

To check whether a plant needs watering, use the classic digital watering device, your finger. If the compost is dry at a depth of 2.5cm/1in, it's time to water. Give plants a good soaking, rather than a token splash, but if there's still water in the saucer fifteen minutes later, drain it off.

Reduce watering over winter for all except the cheery seasonal flowering plants. Houseplants are semi-dormant during these darker months and make little new growth.

Most plants can be watered from the top, but there are a few exceptions. Cyclamens grow from a saucer-shaped corm, which can gather water, and hairy-leaved plants such as African violets can also trap water which will cause rotting. In all these cases, water into the saucer until the surface of the compost is moist and tip away any excess.

Houseplants should be fed fortnightly from March to September. While specific houseplant fertilisers can be used, a general one such as Phostrogen will suit them fine.

REPOTTING

Houseplants will outgrow their pots after a time. If you suspect this is the case, lift the plant gently from the pot and inspect the roots. If they're emerging from the holes at the base, or desperately circling round the rootball (seeking fresh soil) the plant should be repotted while it's growing strongly, in spring and early summer.

Using a houseplant or multipurpose compost, put a little in the base of a pot that's only one or two sizes larger than the original. Pop in your plant and fill in around the edges, avoiding air pockets. Firm the compost down, then water well.

Do not be tempted to just plonk the plant in a very large pot and hope that it will grow away even faster. Sadly, what actually happens is that the surplus soil stays soggy and stagnant after watering, causing root rots and the collapse of your precious plant.

TROUBLESHOOTING

That old chestnut about talking to your plants does make some sense, because at the same time you'll be subconsciously checking them over. A few dead or yellowing leaves to be removed, a little colony of greenfly to be dispatched, droopiness indicating lack of water. All potential problems that you can (pardon the pun) nip in the bud.

Greenfly and **whitefly** are the major houseplant pests. Greenfly will quickly succumb to an insecticide spray such as Phostrogen Safer's, but whitefly are more persistent. One of the most effective methods is to suck them off with a hand-held vacuum cleaner.

Scale insects are more easily overlooked, clinging to leaves and stems like tiny limpets. They're pretty resistant to sprays, so use a suitable systemic insecticide.

Red spiders are too small to spot, but you'll see the characteristic pale leaf mottling and very fine webs. Instead of spraying, which doesn't always work, change the conditions in which the plant is growing. Red spiders love dryness, so mist the plant regularly or stand it on a water-filled saucer of gravel to increase humidity.

Mealy bugs are grey-white insects rather like tiny armadillos, often living under a disguise of white fluff. Insecticide is reasonably effective, but they can also be picked off, using a cotton bud dipped in methylated spirits.

Wilting is a sign of either dryness or, more often, overwatering, so check the compost.

Spindly growth means that you haven't been feeding the poor thing, or that it's in too dark a position.

Brown crispy edges on the leaves are normally a response to hot, dry air.

Leaf drop or **bud drop** means that the plant has received some sort of minor shock – a change of position, a cold draught, a period of dryness.

HOLIDAY CARE

At holiday time, most houseplants are perfectly OK without water for a week or so at normal summer temperatures, so long as you water well beforehand and move them to a shady position, but for longer absences you'll need to pre-plan.

If it's a fortnight's holiday, then the bath technique will keep them happy. Water the plants, then line the bath with saturated newspaper or old towels. Group the plants together in the bath, where they should stay nicely damp. If it's a sunny bathroom, give a little shade by half-closing the blinds or curtains.

For longer holidays, you could invest in some capillary matting. The plants are grouped on the matting, which constantly draws water from a reservoir as they need it. The simplest way of doing this is to set plants and matting on a draining board, trailing the end of the matting into a water-filled sink. A similar system can be devised for the bath, setting the plants on upturned plastic seedtrays above the water.

Making the most of Gift plants

For Christmas and Mother's Day, garden centres are bursting with bright flowering plants – welcome gifts, but they do need a little care to keep them at their best.

POINSETTIAS

Poinsettias like a warm, well-lit spot, and a compost that's kept just moist. Most people discard them once the red bracts have fallen, but if you fancy a challenge, grow them on for the following Christmas. In late March, leave the plant unwatered for three weeks, then cut it back to 10cm/4in and water and feed as normal through summer. To produce red bracts again, keep the plant in total darkness (by covering with a black polythene bag, or putting it in a cupboard) from 6pm to 8am, for a period of eight weeks starting in September.

AZALEAS

Azaleas also thrive in warmth and light, but it's essential to keep the compost moist at all times. These are lime-hating plants, so if you're in

Cyclamen persicum

Euphorbia pulcherrima *(Poinsettia)*

a hard water area, use fresh rainwater or boiled (then cooled!) water. In May, after the last frosts, repot if necessary and sink the pot in a shady spot in the garden, watering and feeding regularly. Bring indoors in autumn, move into a slightly larger pot using ericaceous (lime-free) compost and, fingers crossed, you should have another fine show of flowers.

CYCLAMENS

Cyclamens are often regarded as temporary plants, but we know of one which has flourished for a staggering 54 years. The secret is keep them as cool as possible without letting them freeze (an unheated porch or conservatory is ideal). A fortnightly feed will prolong flowering, often for

several months. They will begin to go dormant after flowering, so gradually reduce watering until they're completely dry and store in a cool dry place. New growth should start in June or July and you can pot them into fresh compost and begin to water again.

TEMPORARY PLANTS

Chrysanthemums and cinerarias also appreciate cool conditions, which will keep them in flower production for several weeks. They are, however, once-only plants, and should be discarded after flowering.

Equally temporary are the very pretty mixed arrangements in baskets and bowls – they're crammed so full that the plants will soon exhaust the compost. Admire them for a few weeks, but then carefully split them up and put them into individual pots.

A delightful gift basket of ivy and African violets.

Top Ten Houseplants

❀ BEGONIA

The popular flowering begonias are available all year round but it's difficult to persuade them into flower a second time. However, the 'fancy-leaved' *Begonia rex* varieties will keep you cheerful all year. These are splendid, easy plants with striking

GROWING TIPS

✔ *Houseplants hate to be choked with dust, so clean them now and again. Glossy leaved plants can be given a shower, then buffed up with a soft tissue, while spiny characters like cacti, and hairy creatures such as African violets, can be gently cleaned with a dust brush.*

✔ *Once peat-based composts have dried out completely, it's often difficult to re-wet them by conventional watering. Plunge the pots to the rim in a bowl of water until thoroughly saturated, then let any surplus water drain away.*

✔ *When repotting your plants you'll find that some, like African violets, have produced a number of plantlets or offsets. These can be gently pulled away from the parent plant and planted up in individual small pots.*

✔ *With children and pets in mind, it pays to be aware of any houseplants that can cause problems, though garden centre labelling is improving. The only really tricky ones are* Dieffenbachia *(dumb cane) and* Brugmansia *(datura, or angel's trumpet), all parts of which are highly poisonous. Skin rashes can result from handling* Primula obconica *and hyacinth bulbs, though the majority of people are unaffected.*

variegations to the large leaves. The showiest of all has a deep maroon centre surrounded by stripes of pink, silver and white-spotted green, and a purple edge. If potted on regularly, they make remarkable feature plants in a bright spot.

❀ CYPERUS
(Umbrella plant)

Wonderfully architectural, with tall arching stems (to 90cm/3ft) and a topknot of narrow leaves which spread like a many-spoked umbrella. Lovely on a light (but not sunny) window, and the easiest of all houseplants to grow – all you have to do is remember to keep it standing in water, to the rim, at all times. So just set it in an outer pot without drainage holes, and keep topping it up. It's so vigorous that you'll probably have to divide it each spring (sawing through the matted roots with a large knife).

❀ CHLOROPHYTUM
(Spider plant)

With their fountains of narrow white-striped leaves and long trailing stems studded with perfectly formed plantlets, spider plants are justifiably popular. They do best in a light airy position, and should be repotted each spring to keep them at their best. They're great plants for hanging baskets and will enjoy a summer holiday in the garden, so long as you keep them well watered. Plantlets can be detached and grown on in small pots.

❀ DRACAENA

Sometimes called dragon plants, dracaenas are handsome

Spathiphyllum *(Peace lily)*

houseplants, with arching sword-shaped leaves on tall stems. Some are attractively striped, one of the finest being tricolor, with very narrow leaves edged in cream and red. Dracaenas have ambitions to be trees and will eventually shed the lower leaves, to form a trunk – a mature multi-stemmed plant is an impressive sight. To keep them at their best, give them a warm room, a moist atmosphere and plenty of light.

❀ FERNS

The Boston fern *(Nephrolepis)* is spectacular, forming dense rosettes of deeply divided light green fronds, 60cm/2ft and more across. They will grow in partial shade, and the key to success is to keep them well watered at all times, in a humid atmosphere – a steamy bathroom suits them well. The bird's nest fern *(Asplenium)* can reach similar proportions, with the glossy undivided apple-green fronds arranged in a shuttlecock pattern; a lovely fern for a shady spot. The dainty maidenhair fern *(Adiantium)* is one of the most tempting, but you should try to resist – it is fiendishly difficult to grow.

❀ FICUS BENJAMINA (Weeping fig)

This is the finest of a large family of plants which range from the tiny creeping fig (Ficus pumila) to the sternly upright rubber plant (Ficus elastica). The semi-weeping branches and glossy leaves make this one of the most decorative of all houseplants, especially in the variegated forms. But they do hate to be moved. As likely as not, yours will shed a heap of leaves when you get it home; don't worry – as long as it has a warm bright spot, free from draughts, it will quickly recover. Water regularly in summer, but it's essential to keep it on the dry side in winter.

❀ HOWEIA (Kentia palm)

If you have a large room and a deep pocket, invest in a Kentia palm; they're breathtakingly elegant. The gracefully arching stems, topped with generous fans of leaves, can reach a height of 3m/10ft and a spread of 2.4m/8ft. Useful, too, because they tolerate partial shade so don't necessarily have to be close to a window. Set yours by a chair so that you can sit under it and dream of far-away places.

❀ SCHEFFLERA (Parasol plant)

Scheffleras are densely bushy plants, covered in umbrellas of fingered glossy leaves, and can grow to more than 1.8m/6ft. Both the plain green and the gold-variegated forms are equally tough, and this is one of the least demanding of all houseplants, so long as it has a reasonably light position. If yours becomes leggy, or has ambitions to reach the ceiling, just cut it back, above a leaf joint, in spring.

❀ SPATHIPHYLLUM (Peace lily)

The white hooded flowers of the peace lily are at their most plentiful in early summer, but are also produced at intervals throughout the year. Even when not in flower, it's a good looking plant, with spear-shaped glossy leaves to a height of 60cm/2ft. Give it a well-lit spot and lots of moisture. This last is vital, so don't let it dry out between waterings, and place it on a water-filled saucer of gravel to keep the atmosphere damp.

❀ YUCCA

Indoor yuccas are close relatives of the popular spiky-leaved garden plants. As they grow the lower leaves die off, until a quite substantial trunk has formed. If yours has outgrown its position, remove the top, pot it up and keep it just moist; the chances are that it will root, as will any stem sections. Yuccas like a well-lit position, and should be allowed to dry out between waterings. Most varieties produce sharp spines at the tips of the leaves which (for safety's sake) can be snipped off without harming the plant.

IDEAS FOR LOW-MAINTENANCE

✔ To reduce watering, group your plants together – water evaporates from the leaves, so that a group will create its own moist microclimate. When repotting, mix water retaining crystals (from a garden centre) with fresh compost.

✔ Phostrogen Plant Pins are an excellent way of keeping houseplants free of pests. They contain a systemic insecticide which is constantly released, and protects plants over a long period.

✔ Airplants are the ultimate in low maintenance. These are jungle plants which cling to trees by their roots, taking in moisture through the leaves. Secure your plant to a piece of wood, and mist daily with rainwater or boiled and cooled tapwater, giving a very dilute liquid feed at fortnightly intervals through summer.

Boston fern
Urn plant
Pineapple
Parasol plant
Swiss cheese plant
Asparagus fern

Lawns

It's a strange thing really. The lawn sits quietly growing and we tend to take it for granted, yet it's one of the most important features of all – the perfect green backdrop for the rest of the garden. As professional gardeners learn early in their career, if the lawn looks good, it has a remarkable ability to make everything else look that much better too.

So even if you do consider it just as a play area for the kids or a place to pitch your deckchair, it's worth spending a little time caring for it. We're not going to bully you into making a bowling green lawn – just something perfectly acceptable and good looking. It won't be quite Wimbledon quality (you need the top seeds for that!), but it will be a lawn that will do you proud.

GROWING SUCCESS
STARTING FROM SCRATCH
Turf or seed? Turf gives (almost) instant results, but is relatively expensive and quite heavy work. Seed is much cheaper, easier to use on irregularly shaped lawns, available in a wider range of mixes and far lighter work. But it takes three or four months to establish and needs careful looking after in the early stages.

GETTING GOING
Whether you decide on turf or seed, the key to a good lawn is to prepare the ground well – it may seem an awful chore (it is) but you'll end up with a far better lawn which is unlikely to present long-term problems.

First clear the ground of any weeds or existing grass. It's particularly important to get rid of perennial weeds such as couch grass, so apply a systemic weedkiller like Round-up or Tumbleweed, which doesn't persist in the soil. Once the weeds have died back after four weeks or so, they can be raked away.

Dig over (or rotavate) the area, incorporating plenty of organic matter such as well rotted horse manure if the soil is poor. If it's really heavy, fork in lots of gravel or grit to improve the drainage. Roughly rake the area level and

This simple circular sweep of lawn echoes the patio design and will be relatively easy to maintain.

remove any large stones, then firm it down by going over the whole patch taking small steps and rocking back on your heels (the neighbours will think you've gone dotty, but never mind).

Next, lightly rake the top surface, evening out any humps or hollows, until you're satisfied that it's level – you can always double check with a plank and a spirit level. Finally, rake in a general fertiliser like Growmore at 1.5oz per sq yd/50g per sq m, a couple of days before turfing or seeding.

SOWING GRASS SEED
Early autumn is the best time to sow seed – spring is fine too, but you'll have to weed and water more while the grass is establishing.

Grass seed comes in a variety of mixes including those for hard wear (ideal for a family lawn), for shade, and for the bowling green look. Wide leaved grasses are used for the hardest wear, with very fine grasses reserved for purely ornamental lawns which need a great deal more care and attention.

The most even way to sow is to use a machine from the garden centre or hire shop. Measure out the quantity of seed needed for the area, following the pack instructions to the letter – too little seed means a sparse cover, too much can cause overcrowding and the possibility of disease. Use half the seed to sow the area in one direction, and the remainder at right angles to the first sowing, to get an even cover.

If you're sowing by hand, divide the area into sections approximately 90cm/3ft square, using string and pegs or bamboo canes. Weigh out the quantity needed for one section, divide it in half and put it in a plastic cup. Shake the seed level and mark this level on the inside of the cup, so that you can simply refill it rather than weighing the seed each time. Working in one section at a time, sow half the seed in one direction and the rest at right angles.

After sowing, lightly rake the seed into the soil surface and water thoroughly, using a sprinkler. If birds are likely to be a problem, cover the area with fine mesh plastic netting or string decorated with strips of silver foil, or get a cat.

Germination should start in 7-21 days and it's important to keep the plot watered in dry weather. When the grass is 2.5cm/1in high, remove the bird deterrents (but keep the cat) and when it reaches 5cm/2in give it a light trim back to 2.5cm/1in. Rake up

Newly sown or turfed lawns should be kept well watered for the first two or three months.

Individual turves should be butted tightly together, and any small gaps filled with compost.

the clippings if the mower doesn't have a grass box and continue mowing as needed, keeping the height at 2.5cm/1in. Once the grass is well established, you can begin to mow rather more closely.

Any weeds should be dealt with quickly before they swamp the grass seedlings. Annual weeds are killed by mowing, but perennials such as dandelions and docks should be carefully dug out while they're still small. And although it's tempting, try to keep off the lawn for the first three or four months so that you don't damage the young grasses.

LAYING TURF

Turf can be laid at any time of year so long as the ground isn't bone dry, waterlogged or frozen but, as with seed, autumn and spring are best.

Meadow turf (usually from old pasture land) is the cheapest, but can be coarse and patchy, and needs frequent mowing. Cultivated turf, grown in special turf fields, is more expensive but has a much better finish. Most garden centres stock up with turf at the end of the week, so pop along and check the quality.

Turf should be laid immediately, while it's still fresh. (If this isn't possible, spread out the turves, grass side up, and keep them well watered for a maximum of two days.) Lay the first row of turves in a straight line, butting the edges together, then offset the turves of subsequent rows so that the finished effect is rather like bricks in a wall.

Finally, trim the edges to shape. For a curved edge, use a hosepipe to make the outline; for a straight edge, stretch taut string between pegs then align a plank with it and use it as a ruler. You can use a spade to cut the edges, but a sharp knife makes a neater job.

RENOVATING A TIRED LAWN

However well you look after your lawn, constant wear and tear takes its toll, but it's surprisingly easy to revive it.

Repair **bare patches** by sprinkling in 70g per sq m/2oz per sq yd of Growmore, raking it into the soil then scattering in 35g per sq m/1oz per sq yd of grass seed. Rake the seed in, firm the surface, then cover with netting to keep the birds off. Water regularly in dry weather until the new grass has established.

To level **humps and hollows**, cut a cross through them with a spade then carefully slice under and fold back the cut sections of turf. For a hump, remove some of the soil; for a hollow, fill in the dip with extra soil. When you're happy that the turf is level, firm it down and water well.

If the **edge** of the lawn has crumbled away, cut out a square of turf around the damaged section and simply turn it round, so that the lawn once again has a firm edge. Fill in the damaged section with soil, and re-seed.

Overseeding – a technique much used by professional groundsmen – can totally revitalise sparse or thin grass and can be done any time between April and October. Rake the lawn vigorously to roughen up the soil surface, then sprinkle in grass seed at 35g per sq m/1oz per sq yd. Keep it well watered until the new grass has established.

Most of these jobs are best carried out in autumn or spring, but you can attack the humps and hollows at any time of year.

Keep the turf well watered in dry weather and don't walk on it for at least a month, except to mow it. Keep it at a height of 1.2-2.5cm/½-1in until the turves have knitted together, when it can be mowed at the height that suits your needs.

MOWING

Regular mowing creates a densely-covered healthy lawn, but don't cut so low that you scalp it, producing bare patches and weeds. The cutting height for family lawns should be around 1.2-2.5cm/½-1in, but finer, more ornamental lawns can be cut a fraction lower. As to the clippings, it's up to you. If you want a super-fine finish, use a mower fitted with a grass box, or rake up the clippings. Some gardeners prefer to leave them, to help feed the lawn, but this can create a 'thatch' of dead grass on the soil surface.

If you're looking for a new mower, you'll find a bewildering range available. Generally, 30cm/12in mowers are ideal for small lawns and 35-40cm/14-16in models will suit larger lawns. Cylinder mowers usually give the best finish, but rotary and hover mowers are great for longer or slightly uneven grass. And if you want the classic stripe, use a mower fitted with a roller.

EDGING

Although it's a bit of a bind, trimming the edges makes a tremendous difference to the appearance of a lawn. Long-handled shears are the easiest to use, but 'crouch and cut' lawn edgers are cheaper. Alternatively, set a 'mowing strip' of paving or bricks around the lawn,

Using a mower with a roller attachment creates the classic striped lawn for which English gardens are famous.

AUTUMN MAKE-OVER

If you want to keep your lawn looking really good, give it the full beauty treatment every second or third autumn. It's excruciatingly hard work but both you and the lawn will be in much better shape by the time you've finished.

The first job is to remove moss and dead grass from the soil surface by raking it out. This is called scarifying and it can be exhausting if you're using a lawn rake. The easier alternative is to hire or buy an electric scarifier. You'll be horrified at the barrowloads you rake out, and positively appalled when you see how battle-scarred the lawn looks when you've finished – all tufts and bald bits. This is perfectly normal, so don't panic.

Next, aerate to improve the drainage. Again, machines are available, but on small lawns you can simply use a garden fork. Insert it to a depth of 10cm/4in and rock it back and forth, repeating the exercise at 15cm/6in intervals. Have the Radox ready by the bath – you'll need it.

If you're a perfectionist, scatter good compost over the whole lawn and brush it in so that it trickles into the holes you've made. This 'top-dressing' enriches the soil and stimulates new growth. Similarly, heavy soils will appreciate a top-dressing of sand or grit to keep them open and well drained.

The autumn make-over is not an essential part of lawn maintenance, but you'll be astounded at just how good your lawn looks by the following spring.

If the lawn is set below the surrounding paving, leave a 'mowing gap' between lawn and edging to minimise edge-trimming.

fractionally below the level of the turf, so that you can mow right to the very edge.

FEEDING

Grass is as hungry as any other plant and a couple of applications of lawn fertiliser works wonders, restoring even the tiredest patch. The first feed, in late spring, greens up the grass within just a few days, while an autumn feed acts more slowly but helps it to build up strength for winter and spring. Be sure to apply the correct seasonal fertiliser – spring/summer feed for lushness, autumn feed for toughness.

WATERING

Watering is only really necessary in a drought, assuming that a hose-pipe ban isn't in force. A healthy lawn can survive without water for a long time, but it does turn brown and is more prone to weeds afterwards. If you do water, do it thoroughly. A gentle sprinkling is ineffective and actually makes things worse by encouraging roots to grow close to the surface. A good soaking of 10-15cm/4-6in is ideal, and if you want to check this, place a jam jar on the lawn

TROUBLESHOOTING

Lawn diseases are fortunately rare. **Fusarium patch** (snow mould) is the main offender, but even that is pretty uncommon. It generally attacks poorly drained or overfed lawns in autumn and winter, causing patches of turf to yellow and die, and sometimes producing a fluffy white mould. You can treat it with a fungicide, but it's best controlled by improving drainage and never using a spring/summer fertiliser after July.

Moss is usually found on shaded or badly drained lawns. The instant solution is to apply a moss killer, but the beneficial effect is short-lived and it will have to be re-applied every year. The long term answer is to improve the growing conditions. There's little you can do about shade, but you could oversow the area each spring with a shade-tolerant grass mix, to revitalise it for a time. Drainage can be improved by spiking and raking (see Autumn Make-over for details).

Brown patches on the lawn in midsummer, and a host of enthusiastic starlings, indicate **leatherjackets –** the large brown larvae of the cranefly (daddy-long-legs). There are now biological controls available, but there's a cheaper method. Soak the affected areas with water and cover with black plastic overnight. The leatherjackets will come to the surface and can be left as a treat for the birds, or collected up and destroyed.

Worm casts may be a nuisance, but are easily swept away when dry. A good worm population is vital to the health of the lawn, aerating it and bringing good soil to the surface. They should be encouraged, never killed.

Lawn weeds will quickly succumb to an application of lawn weedkiller or to individual treatment with a spot–weeder.

before turning on the sprinkler – once it's filled to the required level you can turn the water off.

WEEDING

Some summer fertilisers are combined with weedkillers making it easy to weed and feed in one go, but this should only be necessary if weeds have really taken over.

Most gardeners take a relaxed attitude to weeds in the lawn, so don't worry too much about 'quiet' weeds like speedwell and clover which blend in with the grasses. More thuggish weeds, such as dandelions and plantains, should be dug out or dabbed with Elliott Touchweeder.

One of the simplest ways of keeping weeds at bay is to let the grass do it for you. Cut it quite high (2.5cm/1in for a family lawn, 1.5cm/¾in for a fine lawn) but do it little and often, to thicken it up. Feeding the lawn, as well as watering in dry spells, also helps to build up stronger, more dense grass which will tend to smother out weeds.

IDEAS FOR LOW-MAINTENANCE

✔ *Applying fertiliser makes the grass grow more quickly, so you'll have to mow more often. Some gardeners only give their lawns a single annual feed in autumn, while others simply rely on clippings to keep it fed. Like housework, it's a matter of balancing your standards of perfection with the time available.*

✔ *If you've a very large lawn you could consider letting some areas of the grass grow longer and develop it into a meadow, which would only need cutting twice a year (in July and September).*

✔ *Save time by using a mower that will cope easily with your grass. Most small electric mowers struggle on bumpy ground or rough grass – a hover mower or small petrol rotary mower would be far more effective. For larger lawns, the bigger mowers have a greater cutting width, so there's less walking up and down.*

Low maintenance

A garden that looks good all year round, yet needs very little care and attention. It sounds suspiciously too good to be true, doesn't it? But, with some careful planning, it's perfectly achievable; you can, honestly, spend more time relaxing in it than slaving over it.

It won't let you off the hook entirely, of course – you'll need to do the occasional bit of titivating. But by choosing plants that virtually grow themselves, rather than picking the horticultural prima donnas, and by minimising boring chores like lawn mowing and weeding, you'll end up saving an amazing amount of time and effort.

HOW TO CREATE A LOW MAINTENANCE GARDEN

First of all, take a long hard look at the **design** of your garden because this can have a dramatic effect on the amount of time you spend on it. The more complicated the layout, the harder it is to maintain. Fiddly-shaped flower beds, filled with fiddly plants, are pointless if you haven't the time or energy to take care of them. Could the beds be simplified? Could time-consuming small plants be replaced by a few bold, sturdy specimens? As a rule of thumb, a strong, simple design is much easier to look after, and often looks much better.

Of course the easiest solution is to have lots of paving. But a vast expanse of grey slabs can look horribly stark, so break it up by replacing the occasional slab with cobbles, gravel or plants. Timber decking is a low cost alternative to paving, and it's very popular with landscape designers, but in our

Self-clinging ivy and easy-care ferns are two ideal low maintainence plants.

experience it can become very slippery in our damp climate, so perhaps we'd better skate over the subject.

Next, think about your **lawn.** They can take up large areas of the garden and while they're obviously more trouble to look after than paving, it's easy to keep maintenance to a minimum. Mowing and trimming the edges of an average lawn of 100- 200sq m/120-240sq yd shouldn't take more than half an hour a week. The most important thing is to keep the shape simple, avoiding wavy edges and island beds or individual plants in the lawn. In one trial, mowing a lawn containing two large flower beds took twice as long as mowing the same sized lawn that had no obstacles.

Edging the whole lawn with bricks or paving will cut out the need for edge-trimming altogether – set them just below lawn level and skim over them with the mower. And don't feed it too often – it'll only grow faster and need more cutting. A couple of feeds a year, one in late spring and the second with autumn feed in late September, should be sufficient.

Your choice of **plants** is also important. One of the horticultural colleges carried out some research a few years ago to find out how much time is needed to look after different types of plants. On identically sized plots, a bedding scheme took 45 hours a year, a rock garden 35 hours, a mixed border 33 hours and a shrub border 30 hours. But the shrub border underplanted with ground cover took just seven hours a year to maintain.

So it makes sense to cut back on

Making the most of Weed beaters

Weeding is the most unpopular job in the garden, and usually the most time consuming. But weeds can be kept at bay for years on end if you use mulches or ground cover plants.

For best results, start with an all-out attack on existing weeds. Hoe out annuals such as groundsel, and dig out deep-rooted perennials or use a weedkiller like Tumbleweed which contains glyphosate. Once the ground is clean, apply a 7.5cm/3in layer of mulching material. Chipped bark looks best but is very expensive, especially as it has to be topped up every couple of years, so use it in the most visible spots in the garden. In less prominent areas, like the back of borders, black polythene or old carpet is perfectly good and can be disguised with a thin layer of soil.

In the long run, the most cost effective and certainly the prettiest solution is to use ground cover plants to colonise the soil between shrubs and on border edges. Once memorably described as the harassed gardener's secret weapon, they're worth their weight in gold. They grow quickly and, once established, prevent most weeds from growing through. And many will thrive in problem areas such as steep slopes or dry ground under trees – positions where most other plants would fail.

To get the fastest weed smothering effect, plant in clumps of three or more, and mulch around them initially with chipped bark to help them get established; from then on, they'll happily take on the weeds themselves.

A weed-suppressing carpet of shrubs and hardy perennials.

Our favourites include:

Ajuga (bugle): Excellent low growing carpeting plants, with rosettes of leaves spread on runners. Many have coloured foliage ('**Burgundy Glow**' is good) and the small spikes of blue flower are an added attraction in summer. Grows happily in sun or light shade, although cream and green '**Variegata**' is remarkably tolerant of deeper shade. Best in moist soils, but still copes well in dry spots. Height 15cm/6in. Plant 20cm/8in apart.

Alchemilla (lady's mantle): A glorious plant that grows virtually anywhere, sun or shade, dry or damp soil. Attractive fresh green scalloped leaves and masses of sulphur yellow flowers carried in loose sprays. Associates beautifully with most plants, and great for flower arrangements. Height to 45cm/18in. Plant 40cm/16in apart.

Cotoneaster '**Coral Beauty**': A superb evergreen forming a mound of arching stems covered in masses of

tiny white flowers in summer and coral red berries in autumn. Good in any soil, sun or part shade. Great for covering banks. Can eventually reach a height of 90cm/3ft and a spread of 1.8m/6ft or more.

Geraniums: Hardy garden geraniums are wonderfully amenable plants and among the best of all weed-beaters. *Geranium macrorrhizum* has pink flowers, aromatic leaves and copes well in dry shade. '**Wargrave Pink**' grows in any reasonable soil in sun or shade and is covered in pretty salmon-pink flowers all summer. All geraniums look wonderful planted with roses. Heights and planting distances 30-60cm/1-2ft.

Ground cover roses: Superb in sunny positions. Varieties like '**Kent**', '**Surrey**' and '**Northamptonshire**' grow to around 60cm/2ft high, flower all summer and look lovely at the front

of borders. 'Grouse' and 'Partridge' are extremely vigorous, spreading up to 3m/10ft, so are ideal for difficult to maintain banks and slopes, but don't flower quite so continuously. The new bright pink 'Flower Carpet' is reckoned to be the best of all; 75cm/2½ft high and 1.2m/4ft across, it's long flowering and virtually disease free.

Lamium: One of the best for shade, where its variegated foliage really brightens up gloomy areas, but just as good in sun. 'Beacon Silver' has silver-variegated leaves and clear pink flowers, but the pick of them all is white-flowered 'White Nancy' which carpets the ground with fresh white-variegated foliage. Height 15-30cm/6-12in, spread indefinite. Plant 60cm/2ft apart.

Nepeta (catmint): Apart from being much loved by cats, nepeta makes a great weed suppressor. Best in a sunny spot, the grey- green foliage looks good with other plants, and the long spikes of lavender-blue flowers make a bold show through the summer months. 'Six Hills Giant' is the toughest and tallest at 60cm/2ft or more. Plant 60cm/2ft apart.

Pulmonaria: Lovely, early spring flowering plants, easily grown in any reasonable soil but best in shade. 'Redstart' has soft green leaves all year round and rosy red flowers throughout spring. 'Azurea' has bright blue flowers, while 'Sissinghurst White' produces clear white flowers followed by large white- marbled leaves. Height to 30cm/1ft. Plant 30cm/1ft apart.

Vinca (periwinkle): Glossily evergreen creeping plant, good in full or partial shade but best in sun. Can cope with dry soil. Look out for forms of *Vinca minor* – much more compact than the ordinary periwinkle, *Vinca major*, which is a bit of a rampager. 'La Grave' (also known as 'Bowles' Variety') has lovely light blue flowers in spring and early summer, and sometimes later in the year. Height 10cm/4in. Plant 45cm/18in apart.

labour intensive plants like seasonal bedding and gradually introduce more easy care shrubs, especially the undemanding evergreen varieties which provide the backbone of the garden, plus plenty of weed-suppressing ground cover. You don't have to sacrifice flowers entirely of course, but try to concentrate on a few of the long flowering shrubs and climbers (some roses and clematis, for instance, will produce a good show right through summer) and add in plenty of those ground cover plants which are valued for their flowers.

Vegetables, much as we love growing them, are also time consuming, and fruit isn't a bowl of cherries either. Containers and, in particular, hanging baskets give a wonderful splash of colour, but can need an awful lot of watering in summer. So don't get too carried away with these labour intensive plants – have a few, by all means, but don't overdo it.

Once you've dug up the vegetable garden and thrown out the bedding plants and you're looking for something more carefree to plant, make sure you stick to varieties that suit your soil, climate and the position you want to put them in. If you don't, it'll be hard work trying to get them established and even if they do grow they'll be far more prone to pests and diseases. Your garden centre, if it's worth its salt, should be able to advise you on choosing the best low-maintenance plants for local conditions.

Hostas and rodgersias make ideal ground cover for a moist soil.

Top Low Maintenance Plants

❀ TREE

A healthy well-grown tree needs absolutely minimal maintenance, but always check the eventual height – they look innocent enough at the garden centre, but some varieties can grow huge and you'll be forever chopping them back (bad news for them and you). Native varieties such as birch (*Betula*), hawthorn (*Crataegus*), rowan or mountain ash (*Sorbus aucuparia*) and their more upright cousins the whitebeams (*Sorbus aria*) are eminently trouble-free. The honey locust (*Gleditsia*) is tough, tolerant and grows well in dry soils – the variety 'Sunburst' is a corker. But our favourites are the crab apples (*Malus*) with beautiful spring flowers followed by long lasting and highly decorative autumn fruit.

❀ SHRUBS

Evergreen shrubs provide year round structure for the garden. Many are exceedingly easy to please, and among the most reliable are: winter-flowering mahonia and *Viburnum tinus* 'Eve Price'; gold-variegated *Euonymus fortunei* 'Emerald 'n' Gold' and the taller *Elaeagnus* 'Limelight'; aromatic choisya (Mexican orange blossom); and in lime free soil, Japanese azaleas. Cotoneasters and berberis will also grow just about anywhere, and hollies make superb evergreen shrubs, though they're a bit slow to get going. Of the deciduous varieties, dogwoods (*Cornus*) give excellent winter stem colour, brooms (*Cytisus*) are free flowering in spring, and *Spiraea* 'Goldflame' is valuable for both summer flower and leaf colour.

❀ CLIMBERS

When buying a climber, check that it

TIME-SAVING TIPS

✔ *It's worth considering whether you would be better off without your front lawn. A small lawn takes up a disproportionate amount of time, especially if the mower has to be lugged through the house to get to it. Front gardens can look very attractive without any grass at all, using paving or gravel and just a few choice plants, and are much easier to care for.*

✔ *If you've a hot sunny garden or very fast draining sandy soil, save on watering by choosing plants that will thrive in these conditions. Most herbs, for instance, come from Mediterranean countries with long hot summers and very little rain. Grey or silver leaves are a good indication that a plant will relish a hot spot.*

✔ *For even better long term weed control when planting up a border, use a weed suppression fabric like Plantex which allows air and water through but stops weeds growing. Weed the site first, cut the Plantex to size and lay it on the bed. When planting, cut a cross in the fabric and peel it back while you make the planting hole – it can then be relaid around the plant. A thin layer of bark, gravel or cocoa shell will disguise the Plantex, and you'll have many years of weed free gardening.*

Ground cover rose 'Flower Carpet'

Sedum *'Autumn Joy'*

won't outgrow the space available, to save having to constantly cut back. The least trouble of all are the self-clinging climbers, which need no support or tying in. These include ivies (*Hedera*), climbing hydrangea (*Hydrangea petiolaris*), Virginia creeper (*Parthenocissus quinquefolia*) and Boston ivy (*Parthenocissus tricuspidata* 'Veitchii'), all of which, rather usefully, grow happily on north walls. Twining climbers like clematis, lovely though they are, need support and regular pruning. Wall shrubs are generally well behaved, though they may need clipping to shape occasionally – pyracanthas are the toughest but evergreen ceanothus can be wonderful in a sheltered spot.

❀ ROSES

Until quite recently, most roses could hardly be considered as low maintenance plants, needing a regular regime of pruning and spraying to keep them in top form. Thankfully,

MINIMISING WATERING

Using ground cover plants, mulching, and improving the soil with bulky organic matter will all help to retain moisture and cut down on watering, but there will inevitably be hot dry spells when some extra watering becomes necessary. Concentrate your efforts on the most vulnerable plants such as those in containers and anything newly planted; established plants can look after themselves in all but the severest drought. The lawn can be ignored unless it turns distressingly brown – a few thorough soakings should perk it up.

Of course, the ultimate answer for low maintenance gardeners is to install an automatic watering system. Porous or 'seep' hoses are the cheapest option and can be buried just under the soil so that water seeps out to the plants' roots. Micro-drip systems are especially useful for containers, with individual sprinkler heads for each one, though the spaghetti-like tubing has to be carefully disguised. Automatic pop-

up garden sprinklers are beautifully discreet, but much more expensive.

All these systems can be connected to battery operated water computers which are programmed to turn the water on and off at pre-set times. But they are, inevitably, expensive, so it's well worth getting expert advice to make sure you get the watering system that's most closely tailored to your individual needs.

A drip-feed system delivers a constant trickle of water to individual plants.

some of the newer varieties are much easier to grow. Ground cover roses are simplicity itself, needing no pruning at all, though you can shear them over in spring if need be. And most of them are remarkably disease resistant, particularly 'Flower Carpet', so spraying shouldn't be necessary. Patio roses are also worth growing, needing only a light clipping each spring.

❀ HARDY PERENNIALS

Varieties to look out for are those that don't need staking or regular dead-heading; two jobs that most of us could happily do without. That doesn't mean that tall varieties are

out of the question; you just have to be careful. Grasses and bamboos, for instance, can reach dizzy heights without a helping hand, and some tall herbaceous plants, like *Achillea* 'Gold Plate', have exceedingly sturdy stems. All flowering perennials will have to be chopped back at some stage, to remove faded stems, but with some it's a once-only operation. Hardy geraniums fall into this category, as do the late summer flowering sedums such as 'Brilliant' and 'Autumn Joy' which provide a glorious display of colour when everything else is running out of steam.

Pests and diseases

A glance at the gnarled and rotting horrors in any pest and disease handbook will probably give you an attack of the vapours and a determination to concrete over the entire garden. But don't panic – for the most part, pests and diseases are opportunists and only strike when a plant is vulnerable.

The best way of avoiding them is with good growing conditions, vigilance and cleanliness. If you do need to resort to tougher measures, there's usually a choice of chemical or organic controls, and the new biological pest controls are an absolute boon.

So take heart, there are plenty of things you can do to prevent pests and diseases getting a hold, and some very effective remedies if they do slip through your defences.

PEST AND DISEASE PREVENTION
WELL-GROWN PLANTS
A happy, strong-growing plant is much less likely to succumb to disease or to be crippled by pest attack, so your first step is to ensure a healthy soil. As we show in our chapter on soil care, however dreadful the soil you start with, you can build it up to the fine, crumbly texture that any plant would be thrilled to get its roots into.

When buying plants, choose the most sturdy and vigorous, and reject any that show the slightest sign of pest or disease attack. And once home, it's important to grow them in the right situation – sun-lovers like lavenders will sulk in the shade, moisture-lovers such as hostas will hate hot, dry places.

Take care not to damage young plants, especially when planting out, and keep them well watered until they become established – any check in their growth weakens them and makes them much more vulnerable.

VIGILANCE
The sooner you spot a problem the better. Most pests and diseases are very easy to deal with in the early stages and prompt action prevents a minor irritation from turning into a full scale attack. A quiet potter round the

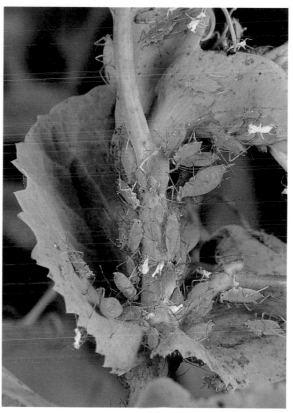

Checking plants regularly, and dealing with pests and diseases in the early stages, helps to prevent problems such as this well-established colony of aphids.

garden at regular intervals, taking stock of your plants, will soon reveal any lurking nasties.

CLEANLINESS
Is next to Godliness and, in a garden, next to impossible. But try to be reasonably clean and tidy. Plant debris and leaf litter are natural hiding places for slugs and snails, and diseased leaves and shoots should always be binned or burned rather than left in the garden to reinfect other plants. Keep the greenhouse floors and staging clean, and always scrub out pots and containers before replanting.

Natural born killers: ladybirds are the natural predator of small insects such as these aphids colonizing a bean plant.

frogs will mop up any that they leave. Nest boxes for birds, cat food and water for the hedgehogs, and ponds for the frogs are all part of the organic gardener's armoury.

Smaller creatures can be equally useful. Ladybirds and their larvae prey on aphids, as do the larvae of lacewings and hover-flies. These last can be attracted to the garden by providing flowers rich in nectar and pollen, such as the quick-growing limnanthes (poached egg plant), a pretty annual with yellow-centred white flowers. Even the much-maligned wasp takes a heavy toll of aphids, and usually seems to be attracted to the garden by jam sandwiches.

BIOLOGICAL CONTROLS

This is one of the most exciting developments in pest control. Natural enemies of the pests are introduced into the greenhouse, conservatory or garden and provide excellent results.

Whitefly, aphids, red spider mite, scale insects and mealybugs can all be controlled in the greenhouse or conservatory by using the appropriate predator. In the garden, microscopic nematodes (eelworms) can be watered into the soil to target slugs, vine weevil and leatherjackets.

Biological controls are available from garden centres, and are also advertised in the back of gardening magazines for mail order customers. But they are still fairly expensive, so take care to use them effectively by following the instructions to the letter – temperature, especially, is critical for success.

ORGANIC CONTROLS

Organic gardeners have many time honoured tricks up their sleeves when it comes to combating pests and diseases. Physical barriers for the low-flying carrot fly; simple traps for earwigs and whitefly; hand-picking of larger pests; using disease resistant varieties; and, most important of all, providing optimum growing conditions for their plants.

If spraying or dusting does become necessary, the chemicals used all come from natural sources – sulphur dust fungicide, for instance, or pyrethrum insecticide which is made from the pyrethrum daisy. Other insecticides are based on soap – an excellent way of cleaning up on the problem.

And the organic gardener cherishes local wildlife as the ultimate in pest control. Birds, for instance, do a wonderful job munching up caterpillars and aphids, hedgehogs can devour up to 200 slugs in one night, and

CHEMICAL CONTROLS

These are man made compounds and despite the current movement towards organic methods, they still have a part to play in pest and disease control, especially if used in conjunction with other methods.

Contact pesticides kill insects, as you'd assume, on contact, but systemic insecticides enter the plant and are taken in by the insects when they feed on it. Similarly, contact fungicides act on surface fungal spores, but systemic sprays kill any within the plant's tissues.

Chemicals are the most instantly effective control method of all, but should be used, we think, only as a last resort. Always take great care when using them. Follow the manufacturer's instructions to the letter, keep a separate watering can or sprayer for applying them, and store them in their original containers, well out of the reach of children and animals.

Pest and disease recognition

We can't claim that this is a comprehensive compendium of plant pests and diseases, but those listed below are the ones you're most likely to meet. If in doubt, consult your garden centre; they should have a plant expert to hand who will help to identify the problem and suggest a remedy. Pests and diseases specific to individual plants (eg. clematis wilt or lily beetle) are discussed in the relevant chapter.

Two important points:

1. When we advocate that you destroy plant material, it's vital that you do just that, by burning it or putting it in the bin. Never add it to the compost heap.

2. When using any proprietary disease treatment, be it organic or chemical, always check to see whether they are any plants on which it should *not* be used. Similarly, check for any harvesting interval for treated fruit and vegetables.

PESTS
APHIDS

Greenfly and blackfly are the most common, but aphids come in a variety of colours including yellow, brown and pink. They are sap-sucking insects up to 6mm/¼in long which attack a wide variety of indoor and outdoor plants.

Greenfly on a euphorbia

Symptoms: Leaves can be sticky and distorted, shoots deformed, with groups of insects clustering under the leaves and along the stems.

Prevention: Encourage hoverflies and other aphid-eating insects. Garden birds, especially tits, will also eat them in quantity.

Organic control: Squirt off with a jet of water or use a soap based insecticide.

Biological control: There are now several aphid predators available for greenhouses and conservatories.

Chemical control: Spray with insecticide. Miracle Garden Care Rapid, containing pirimicarb, is especially good because it doesn't harm bees, ladybirds or lacewing larvae.

....

CATERPILLARS

Some caterpillars are specific to particular groups of plants such as cabbages, but others are far less discriminating and seem to munch anything in sight.

Symptoms: Leaves are eaten, usually from the edge, often giving the leaf a scalloped appearance. Plants can sometimes be stripped

Caterpillar damage to brassica leaves

completely. Some caterpillars bind leaves together with a fine silk or envelop the feeding area in a dense covering of the thread.

Prevention: Squash eggs on the underside of leaves. And encourage birds to the garden – they'll eat them for you.

Organic control: Pick off the caterpillars by hand and squash them or spray with liquid derris.

Biological control: Spray with *Bacillus thuringiensis*, a naturally occuring bacterium which only kills caterpillars.

Chemical control: Spray with an insecticide containing permethrin, such as Bio Sprayday.

....

EARWIGS

This little brown insect, with a fearsome set of pincers at the rear, hides during the day and feeds at night on young leaves and flowers

Earwig

Leaf miner damage

of many plants, particularly clematis, dahlias and chrysanthemums.

Symptoms: Ragged holes appear in the leaves, or the edges of petals are eaten.

Prevention: Minimise their hiding places by tidying up garden rubbish.

Organic control: Place inverted pots, filled with straw, on canes among the plants. The earwigs hide in these and can then be destroyed.

Chemical control: Spray plants at dusk with an insecticide containing permethrin, though this can be rather hit and miss.

LEAF MINER
A surprising number of insects eat their way through the middle of leaves. Plants particularly susceptible include marguerites, lilacs, chrysanthemums, hollies, apples and cherries.

Symptoms: Silvery-white or brown tunnels appear within the leaf. If just a few leaves are affected, this won't harm the plant.

Prevention: None.

Organic control: Pick off and destroy affected leaves.

Chemical control: Spray serious infestations with liquid malathion.

SCALE INSECT
Indoor and greenhouse plants are most commonly affected by these sap-feeders, but many garden trees and shrubs (particularly camellias) can be attacked.

Scale insect damage

Symptoms: Foliage is sticky with honeydew and often blackened with sooty mould. Small limpet-like scales up to 6mm/¼in can be found on stems and the underside of leaves.

Prevention: None.

Organic control: Pick off affected leaves if only a few have been attacked. They can also be washed off, using soapy water.

Chemical control: Spray with liquid malathion as soon as the problem is noticed and again in late May or June. Fruit trees can be given a winter tar oil wash.

SLUGS AND SNAILS
Few pests arouse quite as much passion as these horrors. Virtually all plants can be eaten by them and usually are. Even taller plants are not immune, since they climb to surprising heights.

Symptoms: Seedlings eaten at ground level, new shoots eaten as they appear, holes in foliage and fruit, stems stripped of leaves. Often, a silvery slime trail is visible.

Prevention: They rest in cool damp spots, so keep weeds and long grass at a minimum. Individual young plants can be protected by a circle of grit, thorny rose cuttings or 10cm/4in high sections of plastic bottles.

Organic control: Various traps can be used, like half orange skins, or a margarine tub sunk in the ground and filled with beer (low alcohol lager is best!). Night time patrols with a torch and bowl of salt water are also effective but not for the squeamish. Contact slug killers based on aluminium sulphate can be used but tend to be expensive.

Biological control: A naturally occurring nematode such as Defenders' Nemaslug can be watered onto the moist soil from spring until autumn. Lasting six weeks, it doesn't kill snails but appears to give far better slug control than pellets.

Adult vine weevil

Vine weevil larvae in soil

Chemical control: Scatter slug pellets thinly (10-15cm/4-6in apart) amongst the plants. Replace after a fortnight or so, or after heavy rain. If children or pets use the garden, conceal the pellets so that they are not accidentally eaten.

VINE WEEVIL
Many plants, particularly cyclamen, fuchsias, busy lizzies, pansies and polyanthus are susceptible to this rather secretive pest. The problem can be particularly bad in hanging baskets and containers.

Symptoms: Roots are eaten by a small (no more than 13mm/½in long) white grub with a brown head, and plants slowly wilt and die. The grub later develops into a blackish, slow-moving weevil which eats irregular holes in the edges of leaves.

Prevention: Isn't easy, but as you pot up newly purchased plants, check for signs of the grub in the soil.

Organic control: Remove and destroy grubs when potting up. Squash adult weevils, which are most active at night.

Biological control: This is the most effective treatment. Naturally occuring nematodes like Biosafe can be watered onto the soil or into pots in spring or late summer.

Chemical control: The chemicals available to amateur growers aren't really effective.

WHITEFLY
Indoor and greenhouse plants are affected by several different types of these sap sucking insects, and vegetables, particularly brassicas, are also susceptible.

Symptoms: Clouds of small white insects fly into the air when you brush against plants. In serious infestations, leaves are covered in sticky honeydew and a sooty mould.

Organic control: Yellow sticky traps can be hung in the greenhouse; the flies are attracted by the colour and

Whitefly with pupa cases

come to a sticky end. Alternatively, spray with a soap-based insecticide such as Phostrogen Safer's three or four times, at five day intervals.

Biological control: A parasitic wasp (non-stinging) gives excellent control in greenhouses or conservatories from mid spring to autumn.

Chemical control: Spray with Bio Sprayday at least three times at five day intervals. Unfortunately, some strains of whitefly are immune to pesticides.

PEST CONTROL TIPS

✔ *The New Zealand flatworm is a relatively new pest to this country, and at the moment is mainly confined to parts of Northern Ireland and Scotland. It's regarded as a serious pest because it preys on earthworms which are so invaluable to soil health, so destroy (in salt water) immediately. Up to 17.5cm/7in long, it is dark liver-brown, smooth and slimy and likes damp, dark places.*

✔ *Sometimes companion plants grown next to a crop or particularly susceptible plant may be able to deter pest attack. Strong smelling plants like garlic are reputed to deter greenfly if planted next to roses, and we know from our own experience that pots of basil will keep whitefly out of the greenhouse.*

✔ *Cats are considered by some gardeners to be the biggest pest of the lot. Most of us love them, but they can cause havoc. Sonic devices (advertised in gardening magazines) seem to be the most effective, but they're rather expensive. A cheaper option is putting pea sticks around vulnerable plants. Gels and smelly potions are pretty useless. The ultimate solution, of course, is to get a dog!*

DISEASES

BLACKSPOT/LEAF SPOTS

Blackspot on roses is the most commonly known of the many leaf spot diseases which can attack a wide range of plants.

Symptoms: Black or brown spots or blotches on leaves. Most are relatively harmless, but rose blackspot and spots on vegetables can be serious, so be vigilant.

Prevention: Causes too wide for generalisation, but soil improvement recommended. Buy resistant rose and vegetable varieties where possible.

Organic control: Pick off and destroy affected material. Spraying with Bordeaux mixture or sulphur may help, but is not always effective.

Chemical control: Treat rose blackspot with Bio Systhane or Miracle Garden Care Nimrod-T. Other leaf spots may be controlled by spraying with Bio Supercarb.

BOTRYTIS (grey mould)

Most commonly seen on potted plants, tomatoes, cucumbers and strawberries. Flourishes in damp, cool conditions, on overwatered, overcrowded or damaged plants.

Symptoms: A fluffy grey mould followed by a slimy brown rot on leaves, stems, flowers and fruit of soft-tissued plants.

Prevention: In the greenhouse, keep plants just moist through winter. Ensure good air circulation and do not plant too closely. In the garden, improve soil drainage.

Organic control: Remove and destroy affected parts. Once growing conditions have been improved, spraying is rarely necessary. If it is, use Bordeaux mixture.

Chemical control: Remove and destroy affected parts. Spray with Bio Supercarb.

CLUB ROOT

Can affect all members of the cabbage (brassica) family, and the closely-related wallflowers and stocks.

Symptoms: Plants are stunted and roots abnormally swollen, often into 'fingers'. Spores can remain in the soil for many years.

Prevention: Keep the soil well drained, buy resistant varieties and do not replant brassicas in infected soil.

Organic control: Foliar feed with liquid seaweed such as Maxicrop.

Chemical control: Dip the plant roots/rootballs in Bio Supercarb before planting out.

CORAL SPOT

Most often found on dead wood, but can spread to live wood on trees and shrubs and kill it.

Symptoms: Small, bright orange/pink pustules caused by a fungus.

Prevention: Clear up all infected dead wood, cut out any affected wood from trees and shrubs, and destroy it.

Organic control: None.

Chemical control: None.

DAMPING OFF

This fungus affects the roots of seedlings, especially those in pots and trays. It is most common in cold, damp conditions, or where seedlings are overcrowded and overwatered.

Symptoms: Collapse of seedlings and sometimes a fluffy grey fungus on the compost.

Prevention: Sow seed thinly, ensure good air ventilation, don't overwater. Always use clean pots and fresh compost.

Organic control: Remove affected seedlings and the soil around their roots and improve growing conditions.

Chemical control: In severe attacks, water remaining seedlings with Murphy Traditional Copper Fungicide or Bio Cheshunt Compound.

Grey mould on cyclamen

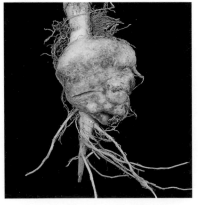

Club root on Brussels sprouts

DOWNY MILDEW
Attacks a wide range of plants and is most active during long damp spells. Can affect densely sown crops, especially on poorly-drained soil.

Symptoms: A grey/white coating on the underside of leaves, and a yellowing of the upper surfaces.

Prevention: Improve drainage. In greenhouses, increase ventilation and do not overwater.

Organic control: Cut out and destroy infected material. Spray remaining plants with Bordeaux mixture if attack is severe.

Chemical control: Remove affected material, then spray with Bio Dithane 945.

POWDERY MILDEW
Affects many plants, and thrives in warm dry weather – especially noticeable in autumn after a hot summer. Michaelmas daisies and some roses are particularly prone.

Symptoms: A powdery white coating, normally on the upper surfaces of leaves and on fruits such as grapes and gooseberries.

Powdery mildew on rose

Prevention: Add organic matter to light or dry soils to aid moisture retention. Keep plants well watered in dry spells.

Organic control: Cut out and destroy severely affected material. Spray with Phostrogen Safer's Liquid Fungicide if attack is severe.

Chemical control: Spray with Miracle Garden Care Nimrod-T or Bio Supercarb.

RUST
Affects many plants, including roses. It is spread by rain splashes and is most prevalent in humid conditions. High nitrogen in the soil, creating lush growth, seems to encourage it.

Symptoms: Orange/brown fungal spots on the underside of leaves and yellow discoloration of the surface.

Prevention: Do not overfeed plants with high nitrogen fertiliser.

Organic control: Pick off and destroy diseased leaves. Spray susceptible plants with Bordeaux mixture early in the season.

Chemical control: As organic, but spray roses with Bio Systhane, other plants with Bio Dithane 945.

SOOTY MOULD
Sooty mould is caused by 'honeydew', a sticky substance excreted by greenfly, scale insects and other sap-sucking pests, which is then colonised by fungi. There is no long-term damage to the plant, but light is excluded from affected leaves and they may die. Any insect-infested

plant can be affected, but plum trees seem to be especially prone.

Symptoms: A sooty black coating on leaves and stems.

Prevention: Encourage birds to the garden in winter to hunt out overwintering aphids and their eggs. A tar oil wash can be used on deciduous trees in winter, but follow the directions very carefully.

Organic control: On smaller trees and shrubs, use a soap-based insecticide such as Phostrogen Safer's. Hosing down helps to remove the sooty deposits.

Chemical control: Spray with a systemic insecticide such as Miracle Garden Care Rapid.

Sooty mould on camellia

IDEAS FOR LOW-MAINTENANCE

✔ *To save time and expense, choose plants which are naturally healthy and trouble-free. We have tried, throughout the book, to recommend only those varieties which will need a minimum of care and attention.*

✔ *Modern fruit and vegetables have been bred with a high resistance to disease, but it's always worth looking out for the words 'resistant to…' on a label or seed packet, as an extra reassurance.*

Roses

It's no surprise that the rose is the most popular flower in the world. Exquisite blooms that can be as richly textured as velvet or as delicate as eggshell china, a wonderful range of colours from the brightest to the most gentle, and unsurpassed fragrances.

Roses look wonderful grown with choice companions, here Viola cornuta *with shrub rose 'Jean Bodin'.*

It really is such a remarkable family of plants that whatever your tastes, one form or another of the versatile rose is bound to captivate you, from the romantic charms of the old shrub roses to the bolder good looks of hybrid teas and floribundas.

Planting a rose is one of the wisest decisions you can make, a long term investment that continues paying the highest dividends year after year.

GROWING SUCCESS
CHOOSING

Take your pick from bare root or container grown plants. Bare root plants are cheaper and are supplied in autumn, normally in a protective wrap which keeps the roots moist and should be left on until planting time. Choose those with healthy, sturdy stems and (if you can see it) a well developed root system. Reject any with withered or brown dead stems.

Container grown plants are available all year, and are the best bet for beginner gardeners, because you're starting with a settled, well established root system. Again, choose one with strong shoots and also with healthy foliage that's free from pests and diseases. But do check that your plants are container grown, not 'containerised' – potted up in autumn and grown on for a little while before sale. Effectively you're buying a bare root rose and a pot of soil so they can be poor value. You'll soon tell if you gently rock the plant; containerised roses wobble.

If you're tempted by a standard rose, make sure you get your money's worth by selecting one with the straightest possible stem and a well-balanced head – reject any with a drunken look.

PLANTING

Roses thrive best in an open, sunny situation on any reasonably fertile, well drained soil. But it's important not to plant them in a spot recently used for rose growing. The soil there becomes 'rose sick' and new plants lack vigour and never really grow well. If you've no alternative because of lack of space, you'll have to dig out the old soil to 60cm/2ft square and wide for each rose and replace it with compost or soil from elsewhere in the garden.

The golden rule with roses is to pamper them at planting time. First water your container plant well, or soak your bare root plant in a bucket for an hour, then dig over the site to a spade's depth, mixing in plenty of compost or well rotted manure.

Next make the planting hole to a depth and width that will comfortably accommodate the rootball of a container plant, or the awkwardly shaped roots of a bare root one – however tempting, don't economise on digging at this stage or you'll have a sad, squashed plant that never does well.

Lower the plant into the hole and make sure that the knobbly union of roots and stem is just below ground level. Mix the soil that you've dug out with a bucketful of well rotted manure or good compost plus a handful of bonemeal, and fill in around the roots, firming down as you go. Water well and mulch around the plant with

more well rotted manure or compost, to lock in the moisture and keep weeds at bay.

Climbing roses can be planted right at the base of pillars, pergolas or fences, but against a wall, where the soil is dry, try to set them at least 45cm/18in away. They can then be led in to the wall by planting them at a 45° angle. The various types of wall supports are discussed in our chapter on climbers, but do try to ensure that there is a breathing space between the support and the wall. This allows good air circulation and helps avoid diseases like mildew.

AFTERCARE

To encourage really vigorous growth, bush roses (HTs, floribundas and patio types) should be cut back to 7.5-10cm/3-4in in their first spring, cutting just above outward pointing buds. Other roses can be left unpruned at this stage.

Keep your plants well watered during any dry spells in their first year, and feed them annually, in March and July, with rose fertiliser. They'll do even better if you mulch them each spring with a 7.5cm/3in layer of well rotted manure.

Dead-heading is important, too. Removing faded flowers helps encourage new shoots and a fresh supply of blooms. Ideally, cut them off a few leaves down the stem, just above an outward facing bud.

PRUNING

Roses are pruned to keep them within bounds, to promote fresh young growth and to make them produce as many flowers as possible. Apart from ramblers and climbers, it's best to do the main pruning in early spring (late February to mid-March) just as they're starting into growth. There's a bit of a mystique about it, but it's far easier than you might think, although the method does vary according to the type of rose. But always make clean cuts – ragged ones can cause stems to die back.

Bush roses (hybrid teas, floribundas and miniatures) Take out any dead bits and twiggy or crossing growths to tidy them, then shorten all the main stems by about a third. You can aim to cut above an outward facing bud, but don't worry too much if you can't find one. Alternatively, just take tops off with shears or a hedgetrimmer. They look shocked and shorn, but the

---

MAKING THE MOST OF CLIMBERS

One of the loveliest sights in the garden is a climbing or rambling rose in full flower against a wall. They take a while to reach this impressive maturity, but you can help them along with some extra care in their first couple of years.

Regular watering and feeding are important of course, but the real secret is training. Once the shoots are long enough, bend them gently in a fan shape and train them sideways along the support – you'll find that you get many more flowers than on vertical stems. As vigorous new shoots appear, tie them in in autumn so that a really good framework is established. Roses trained in this way usually flower well from top to bottom of the plant, but if yours become a little

bare-legged, take out a few of the older stems in autumn to encourage new young growth from the base.

If it isn't possible to train them on the horizontal (in a narrow space, for instance), choose varieties such as 'Golden Showers' and 'Joseph's Coat' which will naturally flower well all the way up.

Climbers grown up pillars, arches or pergolas should be trained in a spiral so that the support is evenly clothed. Once the shoots reach their allotted space, just nip them back as necessary.

With their flexible stems, ramblers are easy to train in a spiral on tall poles. Seen here are 'Debutante' and 'Bleu Magenta'.

Imaginative planting

Hybrid teas and floribundas have traditionally been grown in formal beds, which can look very effective if you use blocks of complementary colour such as lemon, gold and white, with (if you can afford it) a centrally placed standard rose to give extra height. The trouble is, the roses look fine when they're in flower, dullish when they're in leaf, and downright ugly through winter. So give them a few companions to compensate. Edge the bed with low-growing evergreens such as lavender, grey filigree cotton lavender (*Santolina chamaecyparissus*) or woolly silver lamb's ears (*Stachys byzantina/ lanata*), then tuck in a few bulbs for spring interest.

Shrub and English roses are naturals for mixed borders, especially in a free-flowing 'cottage garden' planting. Their gentle colours and full, rounded flowers look perfect with foxgloves, hardy geraniums, peonies, blue or white campanulas and the misty yellow-green flowers of alchemilla (lady's mantle). They're great with other shrubs, too, though do make sure they have room to breathe – they hate to be confined.

Roses mix beautifully with other shrubs and herbaceous plants in a border or a bed.

All but the most vigorous roses grow well in pots, and this can be the best way to make the most of the smaller types. Miniature roses, for instance, can be swamped in the general rush of garden growth and sadly overlooked. But if you put them in pots, and feed and water regularly, they'll be only too eager to display their tiny charms.

The simplest of frames can make a decorative rose-screen.

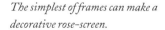

Royal National Rose Society has proved that it's just as effective as secateurs… and much faster!

Shrub roses

As their name suggests, these taller-growing roses should be treated just like shrubs – ie, left in peace unless they become ungainly or overgrown. Every few years, to encourage new growth, you can give them a clear out by removing some of the oldest stems at the base and shortening the rest by a third.

English roses

In early March, on well established plants, take out one or two of the oldest stems and remove any twiggy, dead or diseased wood. Cut back all other branches by about half.

Patio, ground cover and miniature roses

Patio and ground cover roses rarely need pruning. If they've outgrown their position, cut them back in spring. Miniature roses can be pruned in the same way as bush roses, or just given a trim to keep a nicely rounded shape.

Climbing and rambling roses

Climbers and ramblers take three years or so to get established, and should then be pruned annually in September or early October. Remove any dead or damaged wood, then tip back any main shoots that have outgrown their allotted space and cut all sideshoots to 5-7.5cm/2-3in. Some of the main stems will eventually become very woody and less productive, and these can be cut right out, to encourage fresh strong shoots. Ramblers can produce lots of new stems from ground level every year, so that older stems will have to be taken out more regularly. Finally, tie in all long shoots.

Raspberry-pink 'Alexander Girault' and paler pink 'Albertine' smothering a pergola.

TROUBLESHOOTING

Well grown roses are far less prone to pest and disease attacks, but even so problems can occur. The most common pests are **aphids** (greenfly and blackfly) – control them with Phostrogen Safer's insecticide or Miracle Garden Care Rapid. Some varieties are particularly susceptible to the fungal diseases **blackspot**, **mildew** and **rust**, and these can be kept in check with PBI Systhane.

Roses grafted onto wild rootstocks sometimes throw up **suckers**, especially if you haven't planted the rose at the right depth. Suckers are usually lighter green than the true rose, with thorns of a different shape or colour and sets of seven or more leaflets, so they are easy to recognize. Remove them as soon as they appear or they will sap the vigour of the plant. Dig carefully into the soil to find out where they're growing from, then pull them off. Don't cut suckers as this only gets them growing more vigorously.

MAKING THE MOST OF RUGOSAS

Of all the taller shrub roses, the rugosa types are the best behaved and the easiest to grow. They don't much care about soil, diseases seem to pass them by. And they're lovely. Small corrugated leaves, sturdy arching stems (with a good supply of thorns) and some exceptionally pretty flowers throughout summer. Just don't be put off by their names.

'Blanc Double de Coubert' is a translucent white semi double, the flowers opening wide to give out their clean fresh scent. 'Fru Dagmar Hastrup' is pale shell pink, single with lovely red hips in autumn. 'Roseraie de l'Hay' has darkly dramatic crimson-purple double flowers with a perfume to match. Those are just three to start you off.

They're smashing garden plants, but can also do a brilliant job doubling up as hedges. Plant them 1.2m/4ft apart, keep pruning out the top growth to encourage them to bush out, and you'll soon have a wonderful informal, semi-evergreen boundary to around 1.5m/5ft. If you don't dead-head them, the fat red hips are an autumn bonus.

The Top Roses

❀ HYBRID TEAS

For many, these are the classic roses – large, showy blooms, usually one to a stem, throughout summer, on upright bushes to 90cm/3ft or so. Astonishing colour range, and many are fragrant. Lots of desirable forms, and the following are especially good: **'Elina'** (aka 'Peaudouce'): Pale primrose yellow – a beauty. **'Freedom'**: Butter yellow, prolific flowerer **'Just Joey'**: Huge, long-lasting copper-yellow scented blooms. **'Royal William'**: Deepest velvet crimson, rich fragrance. **'Silver Jubilee'**: Peachy pink, very free flowering, well scented.

❀ FLORIBUNDAS

Floribundas, also flowering throughout summer, produce their flowers in clusters, giving a more colourful overall effect than hybrid teas. They're also more branched with a much looser, less formal look. Of the best and most reliable varieties, look out

for: **'Amber Queen'**: Large full flowers of bright amber on neat bushes. **'Iceberg'**: White, and taller than usual at 1.2m/4ft. Extremely long flowering. There's also a lovely climbing version. **'Korresia'**: Golden yellow, fragrant and very disease resistant. **'Sexy Rexy'**: A daft name for a lovely clear pink flower, freely produced. **'Trumpeter'**: Rich bright red, each cluster crammed with flowers.

❀ SHRUB AND OLD GARDEN ROSES

Generally extremely tough, with exceptionally beautiful blooms. Watch out for heights and spreads – some are quite neat but others can be huge. Many flower only once, so in smaller gardens it's worth looking

Shrub rose 'Ballerina'

out for repeat-flowerers, including: **'Ballerina'**: Single pink flowers in dense clusters, very reliable. **'Buff Beauty'**: Globe shaped scented flowers, warm apricot yellow. **'Jacqueline du Pré**: Frilly, semi-double blush white, golden stamens, musk scent. **'Little White Pet'**: Tiny, at 60cm/2ft, small white pompons, delicately scented. **'Madame Isaac Pereire'**: Huge crimson flowers, very full, with magnificent scent.

❀ ENGLISH ROSES

An exciting new breed of roses raised by David Austin, combining the beauty and fragrance of the old roses with the vigour, disease resistance and repeat flowering of modern hybrids. Most have fully double flowers, and will grow to around 1.2m/4ft, with an attractive bushy habit. We love them all, but here are a few favourites: **'Abraham Darby'**: Large cup shaped blooms in apricot and yellow, fruity scent. **'Gertrude Jekyll'**: Vibrant deep pink, strongly

Hybrid tea 'Just Joey'

GROWING TIPS

✔ *If you've run out of wall space, climbing roses can be a lovely feature in the border, grown up a stout pole.*

✔ *Roses generally need a sunny spot, but ground cover varieties cope well in partial shade. On a north wall, try the climbers 'Golden Showers', 'New Dawn', 'Felicite et Perpetue', 'Zephirine Drouhin' and 'Gloire de Dijon'.*

✔ *In addition to those varieties we've already mentioned as having good scent, the Royal National Rose Society especially recommends the hybrid teas 'Fragrant Cloud', 'Wendy Cussons', 'Papa Meilland' and 'Prima Ballerina'.*

Ground cover rose 'Kent'

English rose 'Mary Rose'

scented. **'Graham Thomas'**: Rich yellow flowers with a strong tea rose scent. **'Heritage'**: Soft pink cupped flowers, exceptional fragrance. **'Mary Rose'**: Large loose-petalled pink flowers, sweetly scented – one of the most robust.

❀ PATIO ROSES

Charming dwarf versions of floribundas, most are less than 60cm/2ft high – perfect for small gardens. Superb flower power for the front of borders or pots. And don't be deceived by their dainty habit – they're as tough as old boots. Look out for: **'Anna Ford'**: Bright orange/red, a great performer. **'Cider Cup'**: Another miniature hybrid tea type, deep apricot. **'Gentle Touch'**: Dainty hybrid tea-shaped flowers in pale pink. **'Sweet Dream'**: Apricot peach and sweetly scented – a charmer. **'Sweet Magic'**: Orange with gold tints – delightful.

❀ GROUND COVER ROSES

A remarkably useful group. Densely bushy weed-smothering shrubs, some grow to only 15cm/6in high, while others make great rambling specimens up to 1.8m/6ft high and 4.5m/15ft wide. Especially good for awkward spots such as steep banks and neglected corners. Tough and undemanding, most will flower for months on end. The best long flowering varieties include: **'Flower Carpet'**: Bright pink, 75cm/30in high, 1.2m/4ft spread – exceptionally disease resistant. **'Kent'**: Pure white, in large clusters, 45cm/18in high, 90cm/3ft spread. **'Norfolk'**: Fragrant double, bright yellow blooms, 45cm/18in high, 60cm/2ft spread. **'Surrey'**: Soft pink double flowers, 60cm/2ft high, 1.2m/4ft spread. **'The Fairy'**: Clusters of small pale pink flowers, 2ft/60cm high, 3ft/90cm spread.

❀ MINIATURE ROSES

Growing to no more than 45cm/18in, these are tiny versions of hybrid tea and floribunda roses and

Patio rose 'Sweet Dream'

Climbing rose 'Golden Showers'

repeat-flowerers include: **'Compassion'**: Apricot pink hybrid tea flowers, sweetly scented. **'Dublin Bay'**: Brilliant deep red, a sumptuous colour. **'Golden Showers'**: Gold, fading to cream, very free flowering. **'Good as Gold'**: Miniature patio climber, clear golden yellow. **'New Dawn'**: Clusters of silvery pink flowers, fresh fruity fragrance.

❀ **RAMBLING ROSES**
Ramblers generally have masses of small to medium flowers in clusters and make a magnificent once-only display in early summer. They're ideal for covering large areas and their flexible stems are easily trained along pergolas, arches and trellis, or they can be left to ramble into trees or to grow upwards to cover an eyesore. Here are a few real gems: **'Alberic Barbier'**: Creamy white double with a fruity fragrance and virtually evergreen foliage. **'Albertine'**: Large coppery pink flowers and richly scented. Vicious thorns, **'Félicité et Perpetué'**: Creamy white ruffled flowers and almost evergreen. **'Paul's Himalayan Musk'**: Pretty blush pink rosettes, up to 9m/30ft. **'Paul Transon'**: Neat, at a height of 3m/10ft, with flowers of copper-orange.

IDEAS FOR LOW MAINTENANCE

✔ *To minimise spraying, grow varieties which are known to be disease resistant. Trials by the Royal National Rose Society have shown the following to be promisingly healthy: 'Flower Carpet', 'Princess Michael of Kent', 'Alexander', 'Gilda', 'Elina', 'Little Bo–Peep', 'Red Trail' and 'Telford Promise'. In other trials, the climbers 'Compassion', 'Dublin Bay' and 'New Dawn' were all noted for their disease resistance.*

✔ *On difficult to maintain banks and slopes, try the 'Game Bird' series of ground cover roses. These are vigorous carpeters that can spread up to 3m/10ft – look out for names like 'Grouse', 'Pheasant' and 'Partridge'. Maintenance is easy – just lightly shear them over in spring.*

Miniature rose 'Starina'

are best grown in pots or in groups in the garden. Here's the pick of a dainty bunch: **'Angela Rippon'**: Coral pink. **'Magic Carousel'**: White, each petal edged in red. **'Pretty Polly'**: Clear pink. **'Red Ace'**: Deep velvety red. **'Starina'**: Bright orange scarlet, miniature hybrid tea flowers.

❀ **CLIMBING ROSES**
The flowers are large and showy, produced singly or in small clusters, and the most desirable are those that flower again after the first summer flush. But do check the ultimate height – some can soar to 9m/30ft and more. Most, fortunately, are much more compact and there are even new miniature climbers which reach only 2.1m/7ft. The best of the

Camellia *Donation*

Shrubs

If you want to minimise work in the garden, plant plenty of shrubs – compared with bedding and herbaceous plants, they're a complete push-over. And they're a vital element in your garden picture, giving height and stability to what could otherwise be a rather flat scene in summer and a bleak one in winter.

Flowering shrubs are a delight of course, but those grown for the quality of their foliage can be just as beautiful. So cram them in, exploit the amazing range of form, colour and texture. The word 'shrub' is dull, the plants themselves are anything but.

GROWING SUCCESS
CHOOSING
Most shrubs will grow in a wide range of soils, but a few are fussy (rhododendrons and azaleas, for instance, like acid, peaty conditions). So always check what grows well in your area – neighbours, garden centres and the local horticultural society are all excellent sources of information.

Position can be important, too – a sun-loving cistus (rock rose) for example, will fade away in the dappled shade that a philadelphus (mock orange) would love. Most shrubs are pretty accommodating, falling into the 'sun or partial shade' category, but if in doubt, check the label or a reference book.

At the garden centre, pick out robust plants with sturdy stems and a good cover of healthy leaves. Reject any that are spindly or have been in their pots for too long – a mass of weeds on the surface and lots of roots emerging from the drainage holes are the warning signs. These plants are probably starved and will need careful nursing.

PLANTING AND AFTERCARE
Prepare the ground before planting by forking over the whole area and mixing in a couple of bucketfuls of well rotted horse manure. Water your plant, then set it in the planting hole at the same level as it was

in the pot. Any roots that have wound their way round the inside of the pot should be gently teased from the rootball and spread out in the planting hole to encourage them to grow sideways rather than in circles. Fill in and firm down by pressing the soil around it with your foot.

Water well after planting, and mulch with a layer of bark chippings, organic matter or even a sheet of polythene, to lock in the moisture and deter weeds. Even so, it's especially important to keep the plant well watered through any dry spells in its first year.

Thereafter, give the plants a boost each spring by applying a general fertiliser such as fish, blood and bone and a further mulch of organic matter.

All shrubs grow well in containers and most do best in John Innes No. 3 compost, which is fertile and well-drained. Acid-lovers such as rhododendrons can be planted in lime-free ericaceous compost.

Domes of lavender are edged with dwarf box.

PRUNING

Pruning is generally only needed to keep shrubs tidy – cutting out any weak, damaged or lanky stems, or any that have become old and unproductive. But sometimes (if you didn't check the ultimate height and spread before planting) they need to be cut back to restrict them to their allotted space. Don't be too vicious about it – it's dangerous to hack into a plant if you're not sure that it's one that can stand this treatment. Instead, trim them annually, so that you gradually reduce their spread, by completely removing a few of the older stems and pruning back the remainder by around a third.

The best time to prune most shrubs is in spring when new growth is just beginning (though you can delay a little for varieties like philadelphus which flower in early summer). Pruning in autumn, while they're still growing strongly, can encourage tender new leaves which could be killed by frosts. Always cut back to just above a bud or pair of buds, using secateurs.

RENOVATING SHRUBS

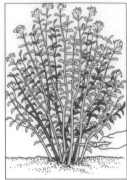

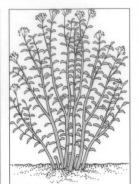

Shrubs can become congested as they age, and flowering will diminish on the older stems. Prune after flowering.

To encourage fresh new growth, cut out up to a third of the older stems to ground level, or to the main stem.

After pruning, the plant will be more open, with plenty of room for new shoots and flowers the following year.

PRUNING BUDDLEIA AND LAVATERA

Buddleia and lavatera reach giant proportions unless pruned hard back every year in March.

Pruning is severe – but worth it! Cut every shoot back to within two or three pairs of buds at its base.

This stimulates a fresh crop of vigorous shoots which will flower later in the year.

BEST BETS FOR HEDGING

The most widely used hedging plant is Leyland cypress, with privet a close second, but if you're feeling adventurous, why not have a bit of fun picking out those shrubs that will make rather more interesting boundaries.

If you want a tight-clipped hedge, *Lonicera nitida* 'Baggesen's Gold' is ideal – a tiny-leaved evergreen honeysuckle that's quite unlike the climbing forms. It grows very easily from cuttings, so invest in a parent plant, stick plenty of shoots in the ground in autumn and wait for them to root. Set them out at 30cm/12in intervals and you'll soon have a fine golden hedge, with densely packed leaves – perfect for creating shaped or topiary effects if you've the time and patience.

For a less formal look, try escallonia, a pink-flowered shrub with small glossy evergreen leaves. Set the plants at 45cm/18in intervals. The flowers appear in June, and once they fade it can be given an annual trim to shape. Pyracantha and berberis can be treated in exactly the same way and will tolerate colder conditions than escallonia.

Lavenders make pretty flowering hedges or edgings, spacing the young plants 30cm/12in apart. Remove faded flower stems in autumn, and rejuvenate the plants in late March by cutting them back by a half. One of the best varieties is the compact 'Hidcote', with very deep purple-blue flowers.

SHADY CHARACTERS

Shady spots in the garden are often regarded as 'difficult', but there are some remarkably decorative shrubs which will thrive.

Hydrangeas can look dry and dusty in sunny spots, but set them in dappled shade and they change character, particularly if the soil is slightly moist. They become vibrant, lush plants, the mophead flowers remaining fresh and bright for weeks.

You can achieve a positively jungle effect if you plant Fatsia japonica in shade. This evergreen makes an enormous plant, with an ultimate height and spread of 3m/10ft, and the glossy mid-green leaves can be as much as 30cm/12in across. Often sold as a houseplant, it will in fact survive in all but the coldest areas so long as it is in a slightly sheltered position.

In heavier shade, lighten the gloom with two gold-variegated shrubs. The spotted laurels (aucubas) are gradually regaining their popularity, and 'Crotonifolia' has the heaviest gold patterning of all – a useful plant in any soil and situation. Equally amenable and brighter still is another evergreen, *Elaeagnus* *pungens* 'Maculata'. Each glossy dark green leaf has a very large central splotch of bright yellow.

Elaeagnus pungens *'Maculata'*

Lovable lime-haters

Some of the loveliest of the flowering shrubs grow best on acid, peaty soil. They will, to a greater or lesser degree, tolerate the lime in other soils, but they'll never achieve their full potential.

Rhododendrons and **azaleas** produce a prolific display in early summer, the leaves almost hidden under the enormous blooms. These are all perfect plants for cool green shade, which echoes their natural habitat and is the ideal way of displaying them. If you're planting in the open garden, set them singly – they're delightful as individual plants, but lose all their character when herded together In clashing colour groups. A peaty soil is essential for rhododendrons, but they'll happily grow in tubs or large pots in lime-free (ericaceous) compost.

The ideal partner for your rhododendrons is **pieris**, which thrives in the same acid and slightly shaded conditions. These are splendid bushy evergreens, with bright copper-red spring growths which gradually turn green, and long dangling clusters of white lily-of-the-valley flowers. 'Forest Flame' is the showiest of the lot.

And if you want a glossy evergreen in-fill to tone down all these bright colours, **skimmia** fits the bill perfectly. Densely bushy to 90cm/3ft, with tiny white flowers in spring followed by clusters of shiny red berries. You need to buy male and female plants of most varieties if you want them to

berry, but *Skimmia reevesiana* is obligingly self-fertile.

The magnificent **magnolias** are less particular about the soil they're grown in – most of them do best in acid conditions, but will tolerate other soils so long as you dig in plenty of organic matter before planting, and apply it as a generous annual mulch thereafter. These are noble plants, and one of the easiest and most popular is *M. soulangeana* – a spreading bush to 3m/10ft, with a fine show of waxy goblet-shaped flowers in April. If space is at a premium, choose *M. stellata*, which will take years to reach 1.5m/5ft or so. The starry white spring flowers are sweetly scented. In colder areas, where early flowers can be hit by frost, try the slightly later-flowering *M. liliflora* 'Nigra', a purplish-pink.

Rhododendron and pieris with tulips and forget-me-nots.

Top Ten Shrubs

❀ BUDDLEJA DAVIDII (Buddleia)

The buddleia's the cheerful Charlie of the gardening world – fast-growing and trouble-free, with long flowerspikes in late summer that are a magnet for butterflies. Three of the best are 'White Cloud', lavender-blue 'Lochinch', and deep purple 'Black Knight'. Buddleias grow virtually anywhere, but prefer sun and a well-drained soil. Left to their own devices they develop into enormous untidy bushes, so trim them back in March to 60-90cm/2-3ft.

IDEAS FOR LOW-MAINTENANCE

✔ *Most shrubs are naturally healthy and long-lived, and a border planted entirely with shrubs is one of the easiest of all to maintain. It can be planned for year round interest, using a good proportion of flowering and evergreen plants and exploiting contrasting leaf shapes and colours.*

✔ *If you're embarking on a shrub collection, it's safest to start with those that fall into the 'virtually indestructible' category and need minimal care and attention. They include buddleia, euonymus, aucuba (laurel), forsythia, pyracantha, cotoneaster, ribes (flowering currant) and weigela.*

✔ *Many shrubs make excellent weed-suppressing ground cover. Low growing varieties will smother weeds out, while others cast a deep shade in which nothing will thrive.*

❀ CAMELLIA

Depending on the variety, camellias flower any time between November and May. They prefer an acid, peaty soil, but will tolerate almost any soil if given an annual mulch of ericaceous (lime-free) compost and a feed in April and July with an ericaceous fertiliser such as Miracid. Frosts and cold winds can damage the flower buds, so place them in a sheltered spot, facing west or north – a southerly position is too hot, and flowers risk frost damage in an east-facing one. Keep well watered when the buds are forming towards the end of summer and prune any straggly growths in late spring. If you buy only one camellia, make it silver-pink 'Donation' – the loveliest of all.

❀ CHOISYA (Mexican orange blossom)

Deservedly popular. Just look at its virtues – aromatic evergreen leaves; scented white flowers in May and sporadically through summer and autumn; bushy domed shape, to

Choisya ternata

1.8m/6ft high and round; thrives in any ordinary soil in sun or dappled shade; amazingly pest and disease free. The worst we can say of it is that in very cold districts it likes the shelter of a wall. The new golden form 'Sundance' is proving to be just as well-behaved as the plain green. Choisyas need no pruning, but can be lightly trimmed back in March to keep them neat.

❀ CORNUS (Dogwood)

The dogwoods grown for their coloured bark are ideal for beds and borders. 'Elegantissima' is the prettiest of all; large leaves generously splashed with white in summer, and a spiky stand of shining red stems in winter. Lovely in sun or partial shade, as is gold-variegated 'Spaethii'. 'Flaviramea' has acid-yellow bark but is a vigorous spreader. They prefer a slightly moist soil, where they'll reach a height and spread of 2.4m/8ft. For fresh supplies of bright bark (it fades as it ages), cut a third of the stems back to ground level each March.

❀ COTONEASTER

Easy to grow, and tremendously versatile. Most are evergreen, and all produce small flowers followed by long lasting autumn berries. To cover a low wall or to tumble down a bank, try the stiffly weeping stems of 'Repens'. Any of the *C. dammeri* varieties ('Coral Beauty' is good) make excellent creeping ground cover. *Cotoneaster horizontalis* will slowly spread its fishbone branches against a wall, to 3m/10ft or more. Cotoneasters grow in any soil, and while they prefer sun, they'll tolerate north or east facing spots so long as they're not too shady.

Lavatera *'Barnsley'*

Spiraea *'Goldflame'*

❀ EUONYMUS

The evergreen forms of euonymus are the work-horses of the shrub border. Pleasant, solid, steady plants which keep on smiling in even the coldest weather. The lowest growing (to around 45cm/18in) are 'Emerald 'n' Gold' and white-variegated 'Silver Queen' – though this latter starts to climb if presented with a wall. For taller plants, choose from green and white 'Emerald Gaiety' (90cm/3ft) and gold-splashed 'Aureopictus' (3m/10ft). They thrive in sun or partial shade in any soil, and can be clipped to shape in spring. Cut out any plain leaved stems on the variegated forms, as they can take over.

❀ LAVATERA (Tree mallow)

A remarkable shrub that can sprint to 1.8m/6ft high and round in a single season, with masses of hollyhock-like flowers from July to the first frosts. The best is the hugely popular 'Barnsley' – pale pink with a deeper pink eye. Lovely for the back of a sunny border, in any well-drained soil. Cut lavateras to within 30cm/1ft of the ground in spring (never in autumn or winter when frosts could damage any new growths and possibly kill the plant). 'Barnsley' sometimes sends out a branch of deeper pink flowers and these 'reversions' should be cut right back to the main stem. They're short-lived (4-5 years as a rule), and can be killed in severe winters, but they're easy to replace from semi-ripe cuttings taken in July.

❀ MAHONIA

Mahonias are tough, and they look it, with sturdy stems and arching sprays of evergreen leathery leaves. They're stately plants (to 1.8-3m/6-10ft) and invaluable for winter colour when the long spikes of golden flower erupt from the tip of each stem. 'Charity' is especially shapely, with delicately scented flowers, but in colder districts, opt for the very similar *Mahonia japonica* which withstands even the severest winter. Mahonias thrive in any soil in partial shade, or in a sunny spot that's not too dry. If any pruning is necessary, do it in late spring.

❀ SPIRAEA

One of the showiest of the summer-flowering spiraeas is 'Goldflame', a neatly rounded shrub to 75cm/2½ft. The emerging spring foliage is a tender copper-gold, maturing to variegated green/gold, with fluffy rose-pink flowerheads in July and August. Spiraeas like sun and a reasonably fertile soil. The old flowerheads can be sheared off in autumn, and if you want to keep plants compact, cut them back to within 10cm/4in of the ground in early March.

❀ VIBURNUM

Viburnums are easy to grow, and vary tremendously. To demonstrate, we'll pick three of our favourites. Deciduous 'Dawn' grows to a stiffly upright 1.8m/6ft, with winter clusters of fragrant rose pink flowers. 'Eve Price' is a rounded evergreen, to 1.2m/4ft, smothered in scented blush-white flowerheads from November to March. 'Onondaga' (1.8m/6ft) has bronze spring foliage, maturing to green, and dusky pink lace-cap flowers in May and June. Grow viburnums in sun or semi-shade, in any ordinary soil.

Soil care

'Take care of the pennies and the pounds will take care of themselves' goes the old saying. Turn it into garden–speak and it runs 'Take care of the soil and the plants will take care of themselves'.

Soil is seen as dull old stuff (sticks to your boots, makes a mess in the house and that's about it), but if you want healthy happy plants that shrug off pests and diseases and give you brilliant results, it needs attention.So grit your teeth and read on through this chapter – of the whole book, it's the one that's vital to successful, and easier, gardening. We won't boggle you with technical terms or complex charts, and we might throw in the odd joke, just to keep you going.

A mix of perennials and bedding plants thrives in well–nourished soil. A mulch of bark chippings keeps down the weeds.

SOIL TYPES AND HOW TO IMPROVE THEM

The ideal soil is as rich, dark and crumbly as best fruit cake. It's a kindly, receptive medium for roots, holds plant nutrients well and is both free draining and (though it seems a contradiction) moisture retentive. If this is what you have in your garden, plants will grow in it like Jack's beanstalk. If you're not one of the favoured few, your soil will fall into one of the following broad categories:

Clay soil: is heavy and dense – when it's wet you can slice it out in neat slabs, when it's dry the spade hits it with a jaw-shuddering clang and won't penetrate. The good news is that it's full of nutrients. Few plants will be able to take advantage of them, however, until you have altered the plant-killing cycle of cold and waterlogged in winter/parched in summer.

Improving a really thick clay soil takes time, but it can be done within four or five years if you stick at it. The key is to dig in (when digging is possible) plenty of organic matter as a soil conditioner, and at the same time add lots of gravel to aid drainage. Do this for the first couple of years, and whenever you plant, but in future years conditioners and gravel can be just lightly forked in – you will have encouraged worms to work the soil and they'll drag them down for you.

Another good way of getting clay into a more crumbly state is to rough dig it in late autumn – slicing out big chunks with a spade and chopping them about. Leave them through winter and you'll find that the frost has caused all these exposed lumps to fracture. You can then bash them into smaller pieces, add gravel and conditioners and mix the whole lot together.

Clay is exhausting stuff to work with, but once you have broken it down to a manageable state, it's one of the richest soils of all.

Peaty soil: is dark, soft and moisture-retentive but in its natural state it lacks the nutrients needed to grow a wide range of plants. Acid-lovers are the ones to start with (heathers, conifers, rhododendrons and azaleas will cope best), but once it has been improved, almost all plants will thrive.

Peaty soil has the invaluable quality of being both free-draining and moisture retentive – the plant remains of which it's made trap moisture, but the air spaces in its construction prevent it from becoming waterlogged. All you have to do is add fertility. So just keep on digging in as much organic matter as your time, patience and purse will bear.

Once you've done that, and a wide variety of weeds start to grow, you'll know that your soil is in good heart,

WORK WITH YOUR SOIL

It's a truth universally acknowledged that if you love rhododendrons, your garden is bound to be on clay, sand or chalk – never the acid peaty soil they need.

You could fight back, of course, creating special peat beds for them, but the soil will eventually win and you'll find yourself tending miserable specimens that are forever ailing. That's how to turn gardening into a chore rather than a pleasure.

So work with your soil type, exploit its potential. Roses love clay – so plant lots. Pinks (dianthus) revel in the lime provided by a chalky soil, so make a speciality of them. Sea hollies (eryngiums) take on an extra lustre in a sandy soil, and there are many lovely forms to be explored. And of course, on a peaty soil you can plant those rhododendrons to your heart's content. To win at gardening, it's best to go with the flow.

And you needn't be entirely bereft of your favourites. All garden plants, with the exception of the very largest shrubs and trees, can be grown in containers, using a compost appropriate to the plant. Harder work in terms of watering and feeding than growing them in open ground, but well worth it for the pleasure they give.

A fertile, well-drained soil is important in any garden but especially in the vegetable plot.

and you'll experience the joy of pulling out long-rooted dandelions without any resistance at all. If you detect a note of jealousy, you're a perceptive reader.

Sandy soil: is one of the worst to work with. It's an inert material which acts like a sieve, with water and nutrients washing through at a great rate. But persistence pays dividends.

Lavish huge amounts of organic matter on it, especially leafmould if you can get hold of it, to bind the sand particles and help stop the drastic loss of moisture and plant foods. But you do have to keep at it – large quantities are needed on a regular basis. Try to avoid growing plants which need regular feeding, such as roses and peonies, and don't even think about growing moisture-lovers. Silver-leaved plants should do well, as will rock rose (*Cistus*), yucca, broom (*Cytisus*), achillea, sedum, mock orange (*Philadelphus*), pinks (*Dianthus*), sea holly (*Eryngium*), crocus and tulips. And it's magic for growing carrots!

Chalky soil: limits what you can grow because while most plants will do well in the top layer of improved soil, some of the lime-haters with vigorous root systems will start to fail when they get down to really chalky levels. The two problems you're fighting are the excess of lime from the chalk, and the free drainage which creates dry conditions. There's little you can do about the former, but you can improve water-retention by digging in lashings of organic matter.

Once you do have a good layer of fertile, moisture-retentive soil, most herbaceous plants and small shrubs will root into it without ever coming into contact with the chalky subsoil. Deeper-rooted trees and larger shrubs are more of a problem, so always check neighbouring gardens to see what grows well. Amongst the better trees to try are ornamental crab apple (*Malus*), juniper, flowering cherry (*Prunus*) and yew. Useful shrubs include mock orange (*Philadelphus*), weigela, forsythia, hebe, laurel (*Aucuba*), lilac (*Syringa*) and buddleia, and one of the best climbers for a chalky soil is honeysuckle (*Lonicera*).

Compost Making

Compost making is the stuff of conservationists' dreams – recycling kitchen and garden waste and turning it into rich, crumbly stuff that will benefit the soil (and your plants) enormously. Making your own compost is by no means obligatory, but there is something very satisfying about it.

Kitchen and domestic waste should yield good amounts of fruit and vegetable peelings and scraps, eggshells, coffee grounds, tea leaves, dust from the hoover bag, the combings from the cat – just about anything except meat, which can attract undesirable visitors like rats.

The garden waste you add to the heap will be leafy or sappy material and woodier prunings which have been chopped up small or shredded. Grass clippings are useful too, but are best sprinkled through the heap – if you add them in bulk they make a slimy mass. Weeds can go in (if they haven't set seed), but don't add the roots of perennials such as dandelions and couch grass, which can resprout. And never add diseased material – most diseases are very persistent and can outlive the composting process.

The neatest way of composting is to buy a purpose-made bin, but you'll probably find that it soon fills up. The alternative method is to make your own, and we'll give you the cheap and cheerful version of compost making (it's not the way perfectionists do it, but it's easy, and gives good results).

Using 90cm/3ft high chicken wire and four stout posts, make a 90cm/3ft square pen, with one side that can be bent back for access. Site the pen so that it's open to rain. Line the base with woody material as a drainage layer. Fill in with your ingredients as they become available, scattering them so that there's a good mix. Add horse manure or a compost accelerator such as Biotal Compost Maker to speed things up.

Once the bin is full you can, if you're feeling energetic, fork out the whole lot, give it a good mix and fork it back, to speed things up even further. And if the weather's very hot and dry, water it to keep it evenly moist. In about six months (in the warmer spring and summer periods), you should have some excellent compost to spread around the garden. If you didn't mix the heap, there'll be lots of unrotted material on the top and round the edges, but this can be incorporated into the next heap.

The natural history of a compost heap is interesting – red brandling worms appear from nowhere and romp about like pigs in clover, and frogs, fieldmice and hedgehogs can also use it for shelter, nesting or even hibernation. So watch where you're putting that fork!

Kitchen scraps and garden waste will eventually turn into moist, fertile, open-textured compost to enrich the soil.

Soil Conditioners

Soil conditioners are used in two ways – either dug into the soil for quick improvement, or laid down as a mulch around plants. Mulching suppresses weeds, retains moisture and supplies some nutrients to the plants, and the mulching material will eventually be incorporated into the soil by worms.

BARK

Chipped bark makes a very attractive mulch, but is rather expensive, so is best saved for 'high profile' areas of the garden. It will last up to three years before it starts to break down into the soil, where it will add fibre and nutrients. Composted bark is also available, for immediate digging in, and has a peat-like consistency.

COCOA SHELL

Cocoa shell is a by-product of the chocolate industry, and has the characteristic rich dark scent – an interesting new fragrance for your garden. The small shells knit together into a tight mass, but they do break down into the soil fairly quickly. They're slightly acid, so are useful for lime-hating plants, and their sharp edges deter slugs.

POTTING COMPOSTS

Any of the garden centre's bagged composts will add bulk and fertility to the soil. This is, however, an expensive option, so use the compost initially for seasonal plants in pots and tubs, before spreading it on the garden.

HOME MADE COMPOSTS

Home made compost is excellent if well made, enriching and conditioning the soil at no cost at all.

LEAFMOULD

Leafmould isn't available commercially, so you'll have to make your own. And it's such good stuff for the garden, adding fertility and retaining moisture, that it's well worth striking up a relationship with a park keeper in autumn. Leafmould can be stacked in wire cages and left to rot down for a couple of years, but it's far simpler to gather the leaves into bin liners each year and tuck

Chipped bark

GROWING TIPS

✔ *Once you are a deeply committed gardener, it's probably worth using a soil test kit to check the alkalinity or acidity of your soil. But for the beginner, it's an exercise in worrying unduly about soil science. Use your common sense, and look at the plants that grow well around you, and you won't go far wrong.*

✔ *Even the best soil can become compacted if you walk on it in wet weather, creating a solid surface that rain can't penetrate. If this happens, fork it over lightly.*

✔ *If your soil is very infertile (if weeds struggle to grow in it, it is), organic matter will improve it in the long term, but you can give it a kick start by adding a slow release fertiliser such as Growmore, Bonemeal, or blood, fish and bone at the recommended rate in spring.*

Cocoa shell

them into a corner of the garden until they're ready for use.

MANURE

Of all the animal manures, horse manure is the best all-rounder. The animal waste provides fertility, while the straw or shavings add organic bulk to the soil, encouraging worms and helping to retain moisture. Well rotted horse manure can be dug in immediately and is available at most garden centres. If you're lucky

Brandling worms in home-made compost

enough to have a stables nearby which will supply it (free in some cases), do remember that it must not be used straight away. In its raw state, horse manure contains a lot of ammonia which damages plants, so stack it for at least six months before use.

MUSHROOM COMPOST

This by-product of the mushroom industry is as good as well rotted horse manure as a soil conditioner. But it does contain small quantities of lime, so don't use it with lime-hating ericaceous plants such as rhododendrons and azaleas.

SAND, GRIT AND GRAVEL

Coarse sand, grit and gravel will all improve a badly drained plot immeasurably. Avoid using fine sand on heavy ground – it can block any air spaces and make the soil even heavier. And don't try to economise by using builder's sand, which contains harmful salts.

PEAT

Peat was once widely used as a soil conditioner, but is falling out of favour because of public concern about the effect of peat extraction on wildlife habitats. In addition to this, it contains very few nutrients so is in fact not nearly as beneficial as, say, rotted horse manure or mushroom compost.

TOPSOIL

If you need large quantities of good soil in a hurry, topsoil is the answer. This is the surface layer of soil (usually removed from building sites) that is well textured and fertile. You can buy it bagged at some garden centres, but by far the cheapest way is to have it delivered loose. But do check it over before it's tipped, because it's just possible you could find yourself lumbered with a heap of poor, stony soil, or one that's full of perennial weeds.

Trees

We know two adjacent front gardens which are virtually identical. Rectangular lawn surrounded by well-tended low plantings. Yet the garden on the right is infinitely more attractive. Why? Because it has a tree in one corner – casting patterned shadows on the grass, echoing every breath of wind and giving the whole garden scale and structure, lifting it from two dimensions into three.

That's the spell that a tree can cast on your garden (and on you, probably), and when you get down to exploring the fantastic variety of shapes, sizes, leaf colour and form, bark colour and texture, and fruits and berries, you'll be spoiled for choice.

Trees really make smashing features, so don't be afraid of planting one (or several). Even the smallest garden can accommodate a tree, as you'll discover later on.

GROWING SUCCESS
CHOOSING

A tree, like a dog, is for life, so do some homework before you buy. Check the label, or a reference book, to make sure that it's the right one for the position you have in mind, for your soil, and for the available space – you don't want a St Bernard where a chihuahua would be more in order.

Choose a sturdy, well-shaped tree that's obviously in good health and if it's **container grown**, make sure that the roots are well established but not congested or matted (ask the garden centre toease it out of the pot). **Bare-root** trees (freshly lifted in late autumn) are particularly good value. If possible, inspect the root system through the wrapping. It should be evenly spread, not gnarled or coiled. The most important factor with **root-balled** trees (also available in autumn, lifted, soil and all, and wrapped) is to check that the root-ball hasn't been allowed to dry out.

PLANTING

Most trees develop a quite extensive root system, so it pays to dig over the whole planting area, adding plenty

Silvery Pyrus salica folia *'Pendula' (willow-leaved pear) makes a striking impact with its dense mound of weeping branches.*

of organic matter such as mushroom compost or well rotted horse manure. Then water container-grown and root-balled plants, and give bare-root trees a drink in a bucket for an hour or so.

Meanwhile, dig a generous planting hole and mix the excavated soil with a couple more bucketfuls of organic matter. Set container grown trees in at the same level as they were in the pot. Bare root and root-balled trees usually have a dark soil mark which shows how deep they were originally planted. Fill in with the soil/organic matter mix, firm it down and water thoroughly.

Unless it's in a very sheltered spot, stake the tree for its first two years, using a stout stake and adjustable tree tie, to a height of 60cm/2ft – short stakes give trees some freedom to whip around in the wind and they form a stouter trunk base, making them more wind-resistant in future.

TREES FOR IMPACT

Every tree has its own character and some are so strikingly individual that they deserve a place in the spotlight, rather than being just a background feature. So bring them into the foreground by placing them as a focal, uncluttered feature in a prominent position such as the centre of a lawn.

Some trees are essentially frivolous – light and frothy, catching every breath of wind. Think of a weeping willow in a breeze and you'll get the idea. *Robinia pseudoacacia* is one of the best of this type for an upstage position, especially the golden form, 'Frisia', growing to 9m/30ft or more, with billows of acacia-like leaves on tiered branches. But don't plant it in too exposed a spot, where strong winds can damage the brittle stems.

Equally happy-go-lucky are birch and eucalyptus – lovely open, informal plants. The trunks are well coloured, too, and multi-stemmed trees can look really stunning.

Then there are the fantastical trees, the curiosities of the tree world: the little corkscrew hazel (*Corylus* 'Contorta'), for instance, or the twisted willow (*Salix matsudana* 'Tortuosa') which spirals and twists, leaves and all, to a height of 12m/40ft – awe-inspiring when the naked branches are revealed in winter. The weeping beech (*Fagus sylvatica* 'Pendula') is pretty amazing too, flinging out arching, drooping stems at extraordinary angles like a demented dancer. Make sure you have room, though, for its height of 15m/50ft and even wider spread.

Robinia pseudoacacia *'Frisia' in the middle of a lawn.*

PLANTING AND STAKING A TREE

Trees are usually a great deal more expensive than shrubs or climbers, and an important element in the garden picture, so it pays to give them the best possible start. Good ground preparation, plus careful planting and staking, will ensure a healthy, fast-growing tree that will give pleasure for decades.

The planting hole should be wide and deep enough to accommodate the tree's roots comfortably.

Drive in a stake (treated with preservative) so that no more than 60cm/2ft is protruding above ground.

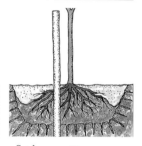

Set bare-root trees on a mound of loose soil and fan out the roots to ensure a firm foothold.

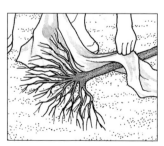

Tip: If your bare-root tree is too big to immerse in water before planting, keep it wrapped in polythene or damp sacking.

Keeping the tree vertical, fill in with your planting mix, firming down with your foot as you go.

Mulch around the tree with organic matter such as mushroom compost and soak thoroughly.

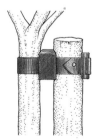

Finally, check that the adjustable tree tie near the top of the stake is firmly fixed in place.

AFTERCARE

Newly planted trees (especially bare-root ones) should be kept well watered through any dry spells in the first year. An annual feed benefits all trees, and this can be supplied as a winter mulch or a spring feed with a general fertiliser such as Growmore. Mulches (of compost or well rotted manure) should be spread 5-7.5cm/2-3in thick, ideally extending as far as the outermost branches.

Pruning shouldn't be necessary, except to shape the tree (by removing low growing branches, for instance) or to take out any dead or diseased material. This is best done in late autumn or winter when the tree is dormant. Trees pruned in early spring when the sap is rising can 'bleed'. When cutting out a whole branch, don't cut it flush with the trunk; cut it back to the 'collar' from which it emerges, which shows as a slight swelling in the trunk.

A few trees produce suckers (new stems) around the main tree, and these should be removed as soon as they're spotted. Pull them off as close to the point of origin as possible.

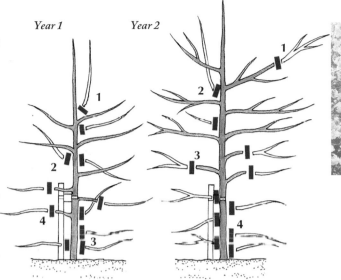

Year 1 *Year 2*

Formative Pruning *Year 1: Remove any competing leader shoots (1), imbalanced (2) or very low (3) branches, and prune back branches on the lower third of the trunk (4).*
Years 2 and 3: Continue to cut back overlong (1) or imbalanced (2) branches, lower branches (3) and any basal growths (4).

TREES FOR SMALL GARDENS

As we said in our introduction, we believe that there's a tree for even the smallest garden and here are six little beauties, all weepers, just crying out for your attention:

Caragana arborescens **'Pendula'**: Feathery leaves and yellow pea-like flowers, to 1.8m/6ft. Requires a fertile soil in sun.

Cotoneaster salicifolius **'Pendulus'** (weeping cotoneaster): Immensely useful grafted evergreen, to 1.8m/6ft, with white summer flowers followed by red berries. Grows best in sun.

Fagus sylvatica **'Purpurea Pendula'** (weeping purple beech): To 3m/10ft, with stiffly cascading branches and very dark purple leaves. Prefers an open, sunny position.

Morus alba **'Pendula'** (weeping mulberry): A curiously humped hummock of a tree, with long curtains of large rough leaves, to 3m/10ft. Needs a sunny, sheltered position in good soil.

Salix caprea **'Kilmarnock'** (Kilmarnock willow): A domed fountain of leaves to 1.8m/6ft, with pretty spring catkins. Grows best in sun and reasonably moist soil.

Sophora japonica **'Pendula'**: A columnar, weeping form of the Japanese pagoda tree, each leaf made up of many small leaflets. Requires a sheltered, sunny spot in fertile soil. 1.8m/6ft.

Caragna is an ideal tree for a garden where space is at a premium.

Added value trees

If the space available dictates that you can only grow one or two trees, it pays to shop carefully for those varieties that give you more than one season of interest. Spring blossom followed by autumn fruits, for instance, like the rowans (*Sorbus*) and crab apples (*Malus*). The snowy mespilus (*Amelanchier*) is also exceptionally good value - a small (4.2m/14ft), open tree, often multi-stemmed, it offers a snowstorm of starry spring flowers, small black berries in a good summer, and incredibly intense autumn colour.

DECORATIVE BARK

But if you want something that looks good all year round, go for a tree with decorative bark. The shapely birches (*Betula*) become dramatic white skeletons in winter, especially if you go to the trouble of scrubbing them down. Equally striking is *Prunus serrula*, a small tree of the cherry

Snowy mespilus (Amelanchier) *provides a blizzard of spring blossom.*

family, whose peeling mahogany red bark is so smooth and shiny that the temptation to stroke it is irresistible. The paperbark maple (*Acer griseum*) is more rough-textured, the old bark constantly flaking to reveal the new cinnamon-coloured bark beneath.

The snakebark maples (*Acer capillipes, A.davidii* and *A.pensylvanicum)* all grow to around 6m/20ft and have beautifully patterned bark, snaked with narrow vertical bands of white and green. Many of the (evergreen) eucalyptus family are also attractively patterned and one of the finest is the slender 6m/20ft snow gum, *Eucalyptus niphophila*. Silvery at first, the bark then begins to peel away in long slivers, forming a patchwork of cream, green and grey. The snow gum is just as hardy as the commoner and much larger *Eucalyptus gunnii*, though it tends to lean, so it's best to use a taller stake than normal to support the slim trunk for the first few years.

One of the most decorative features of the paperbark maple (Acer griseum) *is its peeling, rich-coloured bark.*

Top Trees

silver birch, but this is a variable plant and it's best to buy *Betula pendula* 'Tristis' (approx 10.5m/35ft) if you want to guarantee that elegant droop to the branches. Most birches are white-stemmed of course, and whitest of all (dazzlingly so) is *Betula utilis* var. *jacquemontii* an upright tree to 10.5m/35ft which is especially beautiful in winter. In smaller gardens, *Betula pendula* 'Youngii' is the one to grow, forming a wide weeping dome to a height of around 6m/20ft.

✿ MALUS (Crab apple)

The flowering crabs are an extremely useful and decorative group, especially for the small

✿ ACER (Maples)

An astounding family of trees, from tiny tots to majestic sycamores, with wonderful autumn colour. The best of the very smallest is a large mouthful, *Acer palmatum dissectum atropurpureum*, a shapely bronze-red mound of finely cut leaves to no more than 1.2m/4ft. Another very desirable Japanese maple is *Acer japonicum* 'Aureum', with small golden fan-shaped leaves, taking decades to reach 4.5m/15ft or so. All the Japanese types need partial shade, to prevent the delicate leaves from frizzling in full sun.

If you've room for something taller, take a look at the snakebark and paperbark maples (see 'Added value trees' opposite), and at *Acer pseudoplatanus* 'Brilliantissimum', a round-headed tree to 6m/20ft with typical maple leaves which emerge shrimp-pink and mature through yellow to dark green. All acers like a cool, moist (but not waterlogged) soil, and all the varieties here grow very slowly indeed.

✿ BETULA (Birch)

Birches have a beguiling lightness of touch, with their open, airy habit and small, restless leaves. Tough and easy, they grow on any reasonable soil, in sun or partial shade.

The best known is our native

Acer pseudoplatanus '*Brilliantissimum*'

garden. Reliable and easy to grow on any soil, in sun, they give a fine show of spring blossom followed by heavy crops of small bright fruits. With the exception of 'Red Jade', they grow to around 5m/20ft.

The orange/red fruits of 'John Downie' are the best for crab apple jelly and it's generally more upright than the rest – useful where space is tight. 'Golden Hornet' is a rounder, more spreading tree and the heavy

GROWING TIPS

✔ *Never plant trees too close to the house, where they can damage foundations and even (especially the thirsty willows) break into the drains. As a rule of thumb, if your house is pre-war, the safe planting distance equals the eventual height of the tree. For a post-war house (usually with stronger foundations), the distance can be reduced to two-thirds of the tree's ultimate height.*

✔ *Large 'specimen' trees can be terribly expensive, and although they do have instant impact, they're slower to establish than younger trees which will put on a sprint and eventually catch up with them.*

✔ *Inspect tree ties regularly and adjust them as necessary – a neglected tie can bite into a growing trunk and kill the tree.*

✔ *Laburnums are highly attractive small trees, but the seeds are very poisonous. If there are children about, plant 'Vossii', which sets very few seeds.*

✔ *Trees are sometimes grafted onto another rootstock for added vigour, or grafted as a 'head' on another tree's trunk and roots. If you find alien shoots arising from just below any graft, cut it right back straight away or the more vigorous stock plant will take over.*

clusters of golden yellow fruit are spectacular in autumn, hanging on long after the leaves have fallen. 'Red Jade' is the baby of the family, at only 3.6m/12ft, with a spreading, arching habit and cherry-sized, long-lasting red fruits.

❀ PRUNUS (Cherries)
We're not great fans of the spring-flowering Japanese cherries – they're riveting when they're in blossom, but spend the rest of the year looking pretty dull, with the exception of pink *Prunus* 'Kiku-shidare-sakura' (Cheal's weeping cherry, 4.5m/15ft)

which weeps rather nicely. The one flowering cherry that we really treasure is *Prunus subhirtella* 'Autumnalis', a wide-branched tree to 7.5m/25ft, which produces a haze of semi-double blush-white flowers on bare stems in any mild spell from November to March.

For striking leaf colour, try black-purple *Prunus cerasifera* 'Nigra'. It grows to a neatly rounded 7.5m/25ft, with a good show of pink flowers in spring. Cherries thrive in any ordinary, well-drained soil in a sunny spot.

Malus *'John Downie'*

❀ SALIX (Willow)

We're all familiar with the great sweeping curtains of the weeping willow, but it's a tree best reserved for wide open spaces. Fortunately there's an excellent alternative in the form of the American weeping willow (*Salix purpurea* 'Pendula'), which has the same graceful habit at only 4.5m/15ft.

Another smaller variety worth tracking down is the coyote willow (*Salix exigua*), a multi-stemmed tree with long, narrow, intensely silver leaves, to 3m/10ft.

All willows grow fast and have a healthy thirst, so keep them well away from the house and, especially, from any drains. If you want new plants, just root a few stems in water.

❀ SORBUS (Rowan, Mountain ash)

Robust, undemanding plants, rowans grow in sun or partial shade in any well-drained soil and will delight you with their ferny leaves, heavy clusters of fruit and splendid autumn colours. Birds are fond of the red-berried types, but all the varieties descibed here are bird-proof, and give a bright display over a long period.

Sorbus vilmorinii is the daintiest of the lot, at 3.6m/12ft, with finely divided leaves on elegantly arching branches. The fruits mature from red through pink to white.

Sorbus cashmiriana is another good choice for smaller gardens. It forms a round-headed, spreading tree to 4.5m/15ft or so, with large shiny white berries.

Sorbus 'Joseph Rock' is a much narrower tree, with upswept

Sorbus 'Joseph Rock'

branches to around 6m/20ft, its primrose yellow berries ageing to amber.

Coyote willow (Salix exigua)

IDEAS FOR LOW-MAINTENANCE

✔ *Ferny leaved* Rhus typhina *(sumach) is an immensely popular small tree, but one of the worst for producing suckers, especially if the top growth is harmed. They pop up far from the plant and can be difficult to eradicate. Best avoided unless you have time on your hands.*

✔ *One of the easiest of all trees to grow is hawthorn (*Crataegus*). Usually used as hedging plants, they make fine small trees if trained on a single stem, with the bonus of spring blossom and autumn fruits – 'Paul's Scarlet' is one of the best.*

✔ *For beautiful ground cover, plant* Pyrus salicifolia *'Pendula', the willow leaved pear. It makes a dense silvery mound to 4.5m/15ft high and round, the branches sweeping right to the ground. The dark interior makes a great 'den' for kids.*

Vegetables

Why bother growing your own vegetables when it's far easier to buy them straight from the shops? The simple answer is that the flavour of ultra-fresh vegetables is incomparable – freshly picked and cooked beans doused in butter, tomatoes with that tangy aroma still clinging to them… wonderful.

What's more, if you grow from seed you have access to all the best, latest and more unusual varieties. And you can save money by concentrating on vegetables like cherry tomatoes, mangetout peas and French beans, which are relatively expensive to buy.

You don't even need an enormous amount of space for vegetables – you can grow them in pots on the patio or popped in among the flowers in the border. But we bet that once you've tasted the fruits of your labours, you'll start to yearn for an allotment!

GROWING SUCCESS

Garden centres sell a limited range of young vegetable plants, but if you want the pick of the crops, growing from seed is the best option (see 'Growing from Seed and Cuttings'). Free seed catalogues, advertised in newspapers and gardening magazines, are a mine of information.

Make your choice by consulting your stomach, for varieties that will go down a treat, and your purse, for maximum value – anything that's expensive in the shops, and anything that's quick-maturing and has a long cropping period, like runner beans and courgettes.

For maximum yields, choose a sunny, sheltered spot and if the soil is poor, improve it by digging in plenty of well rotted manure. In future years, this manure can be applied as a 7.5-10cm/3-4in blanket in autumn – the worms will do the digging for you by taking it into the soil. In pots and tubs, use multipurpose compost or (even cheaper) the compost from growbags.

Once they're growing strongly, it's important to keep vegetables free from weeds and well watered in dry spells. Keep an eye out for pests and diseases too – they shouldn't develop into too big a problem if you deal with them promptly.

VEGETABLES IN POTS

If you've a really tiny garden, or just a balcony or patio, grow your vegetables in containers. Even a window box will support a mini-salad selection, with loose-leaf lettuce, spring onions, radish, miniature beetroot or dwarf French beans.

As you'd expect, bigger vegetables need more growing room, and 30cm/12in pots are great for aubergines, peppers, tomatoes, French beans (4 per pot) and runner beans (2 per pot). If you fancy growing courgettes (highly decorative), you need a much larger

pot – anything up to half-barrel size – but you'll get a magnificent crop.

Just as you would for any other container-grown plant, make sure the pot is free-draining, and use a good multipurpose compost. Vegetables crop best in a sunny spot and will need regular watering – sometimes twice a day in the warmest weather.

Feed leafy crops (lettuce etc) with a general fertiliser such as Phostrogen, and fruiting crops (tomatoes, peppers, courgettes) with a high potash feed like liquid tomato food once the first fruits have set.

A colourful mix of beans, lettuces and parsley grow in pots with nasturtiums.

GETTING THE MOST OUT OF RAISED BEDS

This is a brilliant way to grow vegetables because you can really pack them in. Instead of being grown in traditional widely-spaced rows on a big plot, they are densely planted in a narrow bed just 1.2m/4ft wide. All the sowing, planting, weeding and harvesting can be done from the side, without ever having to walk on the bed. The benefits are legion:

- The soil stays open and uncompacted.
- Higher yields from close planting.
- Less weeds because they're smothered out by densely planted crops.
- Food and water aren't wasted on the spaces between rows.
- Easier to manage than large plots – great for beginners, children, and busy gardeners.
- Ideal way of compensating for poor soil because you can build up a good fertile bed on top of it.

A raised bed should be no more than 1.2m/4ft wide (so that you can easily reach the middle from either side), but it can be any length you like. Clear the ground of weeds and dig it over thoroughly, adding lots of organic matter such as well rotted manure or home-made compost, and don't tread on the soil at all after it has been dug.

Edge the bed with wooden board, bricks or tiles – this keeps it looking neat, keeps the soil in and, with any luck, helps discourage children and pets from romping over it.

Crops are then grown in short rows running across the bed. Because you have created high soil fertility with all that organic matter, plants are grown closer together than usual, in staggered rows which maximise the available space. Ideally, the individual plants, when mature, should just touch their neighbours so that no soil is visible. Add more juicy organic matter to the raised bed every autumn and each year the soil will become more fertile and even more productive.

If you're a complete newcomer to vegetable growing, start off with one small bed and see how you get on. We reckon you'll be amazed by the results.

ORNAMENTAL GARDENS

If you haven't room for a vegetable bed, you can always grow them in the borders instead. The prettier varieties, like frilly red 'Lollo Rosso' lettuce, look remarkably attractive (and you can airily tell your friends that it's known as 'edible landscaping'). To give some height to the border, grow climbing beans up a tripod of bamboo canes. The scarlet flowers of runner beans are tremendously decorative, and purple-podded varieties of climbing French bean look positively surreal (but turn green when cooked).

At the back of a sunny border, try globe artichokes, the gourmet's delight. Growing to 1.5m/5ft, they're like magnificent giant thistles and last for years and years.

Towards the front of the border, plant chard (also known as Swiss chard or seakale beet), one of the most striking vegetables of all with deep green spinach-like leaves and fat white or red midribs.

Lettuces can be used as edging plants; loose-leaf varieties, which don't form a dense heart, are ideal for the cut-and-come-again game – just pick off a few leaves when you need them. Chives are good edgers too, forming dense spiky clumps with a wonderful show of pink pompon flowers in June. They'll last for years, especially if you divide them every so often.

A mix of vegetables and flowers looks delightful – and manages to confuse the pests!

Top Vegetables

This is our 'starter-pack' choice of the easiest and most rewarding vegetables.

❀ BEANS

Runner beans and French beans produce really prolific crops in a sunny position on well-drained, fertile soil that has been liberally enriched with organic matter. The easiest way to get them going (especially if slugs are a problem in your garden) is in pots indoors, planting them out when all danger of frost has passed.

One of the prettiest (and most

GROWING TIPS

✔ *As far as possible, try to avoid growing the same type of crop in the same position every year. 'Crop rotation' helps prevent a build up of soil pests and diseases, and keeps it more fertile. The basic crop types are: brassicas (cabbages, sprouts etc), onions, peas and beans, potatoes, and root crops like carrots and parsnips.*

✔ *Sow fast-maturing crops to fill up space while some of the slower growing vegetables are establishing. Radishes, small lettuces, baby carrots, mini-beetroot and spring onions are ideal. If you sow them in small batches every fortnight or so, you'll get a continuous supply rather than a glut.*

✔ *Don't be too traditional about your vegetable beds – cheer them up with herbs, with flowers for cutting and with strawberries.*

compact) ways of growing runner beans is up a wigwam of 2.4m/8ft canes, placed 37.5cm/15in apart in a 90cm/3ft circle. Tie the canes together at the top or use a special cane holder, and plant one bean per cane. Tie in the young shoots as they grow, keep well watered, and pinch out the leading shoot when it reaches the top of the canes. Pick regularly to encourage further cropping. Climbing French beans can be grown in the same way as runners, but dwarf varieties should be set out in rows 25cm/10in apart. Keep them well watered and keep picking – the pods should be tender enough to snap in half.

Troubleshooting

Protect from slugs in the early stages.

Recommended varieties

Stringless runner beans: Desiree, Lady Di.
Dwarf French beans: Aramis, Vilbel, The Prince.

❀ CARROTS

A taste revelation when homegrown. But they must have light, well-drained, fertile soil – peaty or sandy soils are perfect, clay or waterlogged soils are impossible. Sow the seeds thinly in rows 15cm/6in apart. For continuous cropping, sow short rows every 2-3 weeks from March to July. Thin the seedlings to 2.5cm/1in apart and keep well watered.

Troubleshooting

The tunnelling larvae of the carrot fly is the most serious pest. The flies are attracted by the smell of the carrots, so disguise it by planting strong-scented onions or garlic nearby, and thin out seedlings in the evening when the flies are less active. They also tend to fly very close to the ground, so a 60-90cm/2-3ft high barrier of plastic sheeting around the crop will keep them out. A few varieties like 'Fly Away' and 'Sytan' have some resistance to the pest.

Freshly harvested carrots

Recommended varieties
Amsterdam Forcing, Chantenay Red Cored, Early French Frame, Fly Away, Sytan.

❀ COURGETTES and MARROWS

It's a bit of a marketing con, calling them different things, since courgettes are simply baby marrows, but let it pass.

Sow seeds indoors in mid-April or buy plants at the garden centre in May. Plant out when there's no longer any danger of frosts, in a sunny, open site – allow each plant a spread of 90cm/3ft, and double that for trailing marrows. They can also be grown in large pots or growbags as long as they're not allowed to dry out, but are happiest in a fertile soil that's had plenty of manure added. Even in this pampered position, they'll need lots of regular water to produce bumper crops.

For the best flavour and texture, harvest courgettes when they're no bigger than 10cm/4in. Marrows can be picked at any stage from 15cm/6in long.

Troubleshooting
Virus causes yellow mottling of the leaves in mid-summer and affected plants should be destroyed. It's spread by greenfly and blackfly, so keep them at bay. Varieties like 'Badger Cross' have some resistance.

Recommended varieties
Courgettes: Ambassador, Gold Rush, Zucchini. Marrows: Long Green Bush, Badger Cross.

❀ LETTUCE

The best loved of all salad vegetables and we'd recommend that you try some of the 'loose-leaf' varieties that are so expensive in the shops. They come in all shapes and colours, are very nutritious, and individual leaves can be harvested as you need them, rather than cutting the whole plant.

Lettuce does best in fertile, moisture retentive soil in a sunny spot, but are also happy in 12.5cm/5in pots and even window boxes. Sow outdoors at regular intervals from mid-March to late July, thin to 23cm/9in and keep well watered in dry spells.

Troubleshooting
Slugs are the biggest menace. Germination can be erratic in high temperatures, so water the soil before and after sowing, to cool it down.

Recommended varieties
Butterhead: Iceberg.
Cos: Little Gem, Winter Density.
Loose-leaf: Lollo Rossa, Salad Bowl.

❀ ONIONS and SHALLOTS

Incredibly easy and satisfying to grow, even if they are pretty cheap in the shops. Onions can be grown from seed, but it's easier to grow from sets (mini-bulbs) available in spring. Plant in March, 15cm/6in apart in a sunny, well drained position. Push the sets in gently so that only the tips are showing, and keep the weeds away as they grow. They're ready when the leaves start to go yellow. Shallots are grown in exactly the same way, but should be planted in February.

Troubleshooting
The major scourge, onion fly, only affects plants grown from seed, not from sets.

Recommended varieties
Onion: Giant Fen Globe, Jagro, Sturon.
Shallots: Hative de Niort, Pikant.

❀ PEAS

To experience the true sweetness of peas, you have to grow your own, because sugar levels begin to deteriorate just 30 minutes after picking. For maximum crops in a limited space, try the mangetout or sugar snap types, which are eaten pod and all.

All peas need a well drained, fertile soil. Sow them outdoors from March to June, at the planting distance recommended for the particular variety. Most peas need a little support (you've got it – with pea sticks) but some of the semi-leafless varieties need little help. Water well

Courgette 'Gold Rush'

Pea 'Poppet'

Potatoes

in dry weather.
Troubleshooting
Birds love to eat the seedlings, so cover them with netting.
Recommended varieties
Shelling types: Hurst Green Shaft, Markana, Poppet.
Mangetout/sugar snap types: Oregon Sugar Pod, Sugar Bon.

❀ POTATOES
In small gardens, early potatoes are the ones to grow – they're ready when prices are still high in the shops, and they're delicious.

Seed potatoes are available from garden centres and should first be 'chitted' – set in egg trays on windowsills indoors and left to sprout. Plant in late March/early April, 15cm /6in deep, 30cm/1ft apart, in rows 60cm/2ft apart. As the tops grow, regularly draw up soil around them. Keep well watered (essential for good crops) and start to lift them when the first flowers appear.
Troubleshooting
Potato blight is the biggest problem, especially in wet summers, but early

crops are likely to escape it. Dark blotches appear on the leaves and a mould infects the tubers. Spraying with Bordeaux mixture helps, but badly affected crops should be destroyed.
Recommended varieties
(earlies)
Dunluce, Epicure, Foremost, Maris Bard, Pentland Javelin.

❀ TOMATOES
The most popular home-grown vegetable of all, tomatoes can be grown in borders, pots, growbags and even hanging baskets. Keen gardeners grow them from seed sown indoors in March, but most garden centres have a pretty good range of young plants which can be planted in a sunny, sheltered spot outdoors after the last frosts. If you're lucky enough to have a greenhouse, you'll get even earlier crops.

'Cordon' types need to be trained, but it's really quite simple – just support them on a cane, and pinch out any sideshoots from the main stem. Feed weekly once the first tiny fruits appear. Pinch out the top of the plant when four or five flower trusses have set. Bush tomatoes , including the hanging basket form 'Tumbler', are even easier, needing no training. If you're left with lots of unripe fruit at the end of the season, just harvest the whole stem and hang it upside down in a frost-free spot to ripen.
Troubleshooting
Split or cracked skin, or a brown rot at the base of the fruit (blossom end rot), is caused by irregular watering.

Recommended varieties
Cordon: Alicante, Gardener's Delight, Sungold.
Bush: Pixie, Red Alert.

Tomatoes in growbags

Water gardening

Water brings out the child in all of us – there's something mesmerising about it. Whether it's a clear, still pool or a little wall-mounted spout, it draws us like a magnet. There's probably some deeply psychological reason for this, but as we haven't the foggiest what it is, we can only say that water in the garden is a Good Thing.

Japanese iris (Iris laevigata)

Pretty low maintenance, too. Plants will need to be divided every few years, and a thorough dredging operation may be necessary once in a blue moon, but apart from that there's very little work involved. The most time consuming aspect of water gardening is the sitting back and enjoying it.

HOW TO CREATE A GARDEN POND
SITING

A sunny position is best if you want to grow sun-loving plants like water lilies, but shady spots can be considerably enlivened by water and most plants, especially the grasses and sedges, will grow well. But try to avoid the shade cast by trees – fallen leaves pollute the water, harming plant and animal life unless you keep up a regular leaf-clearing routine. Make sure the site's level, too, or the water will look like tea in a tilted cup.

CONSTRUCTION

Preformed plastic or fibreglass pools seem like an 'instant' solution, but can be fiddly to install unless the shape is very simple. Using a butyl liner gives you much more freedom to create a pond that fits your site and suits the garden design. Always use a good quality butyl (look for a 20 year guarantee), unless you want to experience the grim misery of constantly draining and patching a leaking pond.

Mark out the pond shape using garden hose for a

curved pond or pegs and string for a square or rectangle. To calculate the size of liner you'll need, use the following equation:

Length = overall length of pool + twice maximum depth
Width = overall width of pool + twice maximum depth

Dig out the area so that you create a series of 25cm/10in shelves stepped down from the edge – water plants vary in the depth of water they need, and this will allow you to plant a wide selection.

To give birds a chance to bathe, and frogs an easy exit route, make at least one 'beach' area which slopes very gently from the edge. At the centre of the excavation, try to achieve a depth of 60cm/2ft; this area will remain unfrozen through even the worst weather and will protect fish and pond life.

Once the digging is done, remove any sharp stones or debris which could puncture the liner. As an extra precaution, you can line the hole with sand or layers of newspaper. Drape the liner centrally over the hole, then fill from a hose – you'll find that the liner moulds to the shape of the hole simply by the weight of the water.

The gentle murmur of running water adds an extra dimension to this tranquil pool.

Once the pond is full, trim off the excess liner,

CHILDPROOF WATER

Even quite shallow ponds can be a hazard to children, but that doesn't mean you can't have water in the garden. There are ready-made features galore, from wall fountains to water-bathed millstones, but one of the simplest is a bubble pool, which you can put together in an afternoon once you have been shopping for:

- 1 low voltage pond pump with extension pipe
- 1 waterproof tank (eg central heating expansion tank)
- 1 square of rigid mesh
- Pebbles/cobbles/attractive stones

Sink the tank, fill with water, install the pump and position the extension pipe so that it is 7.5-10cm/3-4in above ground level. Place mesh over the tank and mound up your stones to disguise it. Switch on. Water bubbles and gurgles from the pipe and splashes over the stones back into the tank. Magic. Frogs and birds will love it too.

Just two essential points. Water and electricity can be a lethal combination, so always use a circuit breaker instead of a normal plug. And protect any ground-level cable by threading it through tubing (such as pieces of hosepipe), to avoid the possibility of slicing through it while gardening.

A sparkling water feature such as this one in a tub can be tucked into even the smallest garden and surrounded by moisture-loving plants.

leaving an overlap of around 15cm/6in. This is best disguised by a paving surround which overhangs the pond slightly, but in a lawn you can simply tuck it under the turf. Finally, leave the water for a week or so before planting or stocking with fish, to allow any tap water additives to disperse.

PLANTING

Water garden centres stock an excellent range of plants, but if there isn't one near you, there are several very good mail order stockists who advertise in gardening magazines.

Oxygenating plants such as elodea are vital. They produce most of their growth underwater, helping to suppress algae and supplying oxygen for fish and for the general health of the water. They're sold in bunches and you should allow four or five bunches for every square metre or yard.

These oxygenators, plus bare-root water lilies and plants in very small pots, will need to be potted up into plastic mesh planting baskets. As a guide, a 30cm/12in basket will accommodate twelve oxygenating plants or one water lily.

Line the basket with hessian unless the mesh is very fine, and fill with aquatic compost or garden soil – heavy soil that's not too fertile is ideal. Settle the plants so that the point from which the top growth emerges is just at soil level. Top with a 13mm/1in layer of gravel or small stones, to stop the soil from washing away.

Set the basket in the pond at the recommended planting depth (the distance between the top of the pot and the surface of the water), adjusting the height with bricks if necessary. Young lilies can be set high initially, so that the leaves are on the surface, gradually lowering the pot to the right depth as the leaves lengthen.

AFTERCARE

Keep the water as clean as possible by regularly removing any fallen leaves and clear away all dead top growth in late autumn, together with a good proportion of the oxygenating plants if they have become congested.

In winter, toxic gases harmful to fish can build up if the pond is frozen over for several days. Never bash the ice to break it (the shock waves could kill the fish), just set a kettle or pan of boiling water on it until it has melted through. Alternatively, install a pond heater –

cheap to run, and relatively cheap to buy.

Plants will eventually outgrow their baskets and should be lifted and divided in spring or summer (taking care to hose off any water creatures such as tadpoles as you lift). Some roots are easy to tease apart, but others are so dense that you may have to resort to a knife or saw. Replant the best portions in fresh compost.

If a lot of debris has built up in the bottom of the pond, refresh the water by siphoning off half the volume and refilling from a trickling hose. If the build-up is very severe, then the pond will have to be drained and cleaned out – an awesome task that will leave you wishing that you'd kept up a regular leaf-clearing regime. If the pond is a haven for wildlife, leave the bottom couple of inches of mud, which harbours all kinds of beasties, and do the clean-out in autumn – if you do it in spring, you could disrupt spawning frogs or emerging tadpoles.

TROUBLESHOOTING

Ponds are generally very little trouble. It's quite normal for a new pond to develop a green soup look, due to **algae**, but it can be discouraged by using plenty of oxygenating plants, adding water snails to keep down debris, and planting water lilies to provide shade. **Blanketweed** is a spreading form of algae, with long green filaments. It can be raked out, or is easily twizzled round a stick, like making candy floss. The tiny floating plants known as **duckweed** look quite pretty in small numbers, but soon spread – scoop them off the surface of the water with a net. **Aphids** are easily disposed of with a jet from the hose.

Candelabra primulas and Iris ensata *love the boggy conditions at pool edges.*

MAKING THE MOST OF WATER LILIES

Water lilies (*Nymphaea*) are a must for any pond or pool in a sunny spot. The flowers are fabulous and the leaves both decorative and useful – they shade the water, keeping down algae growth which flourishes in sun, and provide a cool hiding place for fish and a launch pad for frogs.

But before you grab the first one that catches your eye, check the eventual spread in case it's more suited to a vast lake than a domestic pool. The aim is to find a plant that will take up around a third of the pool, creating a nice balance of leaf and open water.

In very small ponds, or in water barrels, the dwarf 'Alba' is a little

Nymphaea 'Brakleyi Rosea'

white gem, spreading to only 40cm/16in or so. It has an equally pretty deep pink cousin, 'Rubra', and both should be planted 15-23cm/6-9in deep.

Moving up the scale, white *Nymphaea candida*, to 60cm/2ft, is exceedingly hardy and excellent for pools in colder areas. The Laydekeri hybrids are only slightly wider, at up to 90cm/3ft, and red 'Fulgens' and rose pink 'Lilacea' are both scented. All need a planting depth of around 23cm/9in.

Rose-crimson 'James Brydon', at 1.2m/4ft, is a tried and tested old favourite, but for more substantial stretches of water, look out for the Marliacea hybrids, some of which will spread to 18m/6ft at a planting depth of 30cm/12in or more. White 'Albida' is exceptionally free-flowering and fragrant.

And if you really do have an ornamental lake, chaps like yellow 'Colonel A J Welch' and deep pink 'Charles de Meurville', at 2.4m/8ft wide, planted 60cm/2ft deep, will fill it beautifully.

Top Ten Water Plants

Aponogeton distachyos

Caltha palustris

Mimulus luteus

❀ APONOGETON DISTACHYOS (Water hawthorn)

Extraordinary white flowers with black stamens and a hawthorn/vanilla scent. They're produced on short spikes at almost any time of year, but the two main flushes are in late spring and autumn. The long strap-shaped leaves float on the water in the same way as water lilies. Young plants

GROWING TIPS

✔ *Fish bring life and colour to a pond, but are inadvisable if you're especially interested in wildlife; they feed voraciously on tadpoles, baby frogs and other small pond creatures.*

✔ *Algae can form on the paved or timber edges of ponds, making them dangerously slippery. Clean them down using a scrubbing brush and dilute washing up liquid; never use chemical path cleaners which could leach into the water and harm plants and pond life.*

✔ *Ramshorns are the most useful pond snails – they clear up debris and never snack on pond plants.*

should be set at a depth of 15cm/6in, but once established can gradually be lowered to as deep as 45cm/18in.

❀ CALTHA PALUSTRIS (Marsh marigold)

A lovely pond-edge plant, with hummocks of shiny dark green leaves which in April and May are covered in giant 'buttercups'. The showiest of all is 'Flore Pleno', a very full-petalled double form which sometimes flowers again later in the year. Plant in the shallows, at a depth of no more than 5cm/2in.

Iris ensata

❀ CAREX ELATA 'AUREA' (Bowles' golden sedge)

One of the brightest sedges, and one of the least invasive, forming a neatly rounded clump of gold to a height of 30cm/12in. Plant 2.5cm/1in deep, or in boggy soil at the edge of the pond.

❀ CYPERUS ERAGROSTIS (Umbrella grass)

A close relation of the indoor umbrella plant, with the same arching stems and leafy topknots to a height of 60cm/2ft. Plant at any depth up to 15cm/6in. It's also sold as *Cyperus vegetus*, and is much preferable to *Cyperus longus*, which can be extremely invasive.

❀ IRIS

Grow them for their beauty, ignoring the fact that the flowering period is only a few weeks. There's a vast choice, from *Iris ensata* (sometimes sold as *Iris kaempferi*) which grows in only 2.5cm/1in of water or in boggy soil, through *Iris laevigata* at 5-7.5cm/2-3in deep, to *Iris pseudacorus* which is best suited to large ponds, at a depth of up to 45cm/18in. When you're shopping for ensata irises, look out for the Higo hybrids which have exceptionally large, showy flowers.

✾ MIMULUS LUTEUS (Monkey musk)

Cheerful yellow flowers produced all summer long. They can be grown as a pool-side plant in boggy ground, but are hardiest when planted in water at a depth of 7.5cm/3in. You'll also find annual forms of mimulus at the garden centre, sold as bedding plants, which will grow in shallow water.

✾ MYOSOTIS SCORPIOIDES (Water forget-me-not)

A haze of bright blue flowers from late spring to high summer to 30cm/12in or so. Deep blue 'Mermaid' is especially attractive. Plant in soggy soil at the pond edge, or up to 7.5cm/3in deep in the water. Not reliably long-lived, but seedlings should be plentiful.

✾ NYMPHAEA (Water lily)

The essential water plant for a sunny spot. But awfully expensive, so take care in choosing, and in planting. Water lilies vary tremendously in spread, with some suitable for a water barrel and others for an ornamental lake. But they like a peaceful life, in still water, so don't plant them near a fountain or any other moving water feature.

✾ TYPHA MINIMA (Miniature reedmace)

A delightful small bulrush that won't take over the whole pond, unlike some of its bossy relatives. Grows to 45cm/18in in 5-15cm/2-6in of water. Great for picking – spray the seedheads with hair lacquer to 'fix' them.

Myosotis scorpioides

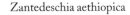

Zantedeschia aethiopica

✾ ZANTEDESCHIA AETHIOPICA (Arum lily)

Stately white flowers to 90cm/3ft from March to June, and handsome arrow-shaped foliage. They've a reputation for being tender, but the secret is to plant them deep – 15cm/6in is about right. At that depth they'll survive in all but the coldest areas. 'Crowborough' is the toughest of the lot.

> ## IDEAS FOR LOW-MAINTENANCE
>
> ✔ *Place a fine mesh net over the pond in autumn, to catch falling leaves – much easier than fishing them out on a daily basis.*
>
> ✔ *When buying plants, steer clear of any described as 'vigorous'; the likelihood is that they will be horribly invasive and need severe cutting back every year.*
>
> ✔ *Unplanted, unstocked pools can be very pleasing – a simple circle of water, for instance, surrounded by attractive paving, makes a lovely feature. In a shady spot, give it extra sparkle by installing a fountain.*

Weed control

Chickweed

Weeds are opportunists, taking advantage of any gap in our defences – creeping along and popping up from underground stems, floating in on air-borne seeds, even attaching their seedheads to our clothes and hitching a ride. Experts in the art of invasion.

They look untidy, they steal water and nutrients, they can choke precious plants, and they're a dratted nuisance. But once you've dealt with the most thuggish types and the garden is fully planted, you'll find that the time spent weeding is reduced to the few seconds it takes to pull out the odd interloper.

CONTROL METHODS

Hand weeding: Pulling weeds by hand or levering them out with a trowel is a good way of getting rid of shallow rooted weeds, and is easiest when the ground is moist.

Hoeing: This is by far the quickest way of eliminating weed seedlings. Draw hoes have curved blades which are angled towards you, and we find them rather awkward. Dutch or 'push' hoes have a forward facing blade which slices effortlessly through the soil surface, taking out the weeds at root level. If the soil is dry, the seedlings can be left to shrivel away – but don't leave them if it's wet, in case they re-root.

Digging: Established weeds can often be dug out with a garden fork, but it's sometimes difficult to clear the ground of those with really vigorous spreading root systems.

Weedkillers: Weedkillers are highly effective, but we're uneasy about those which persist in the soil. Both Tumbleweed and Round-up, which contain glyphosate, are harmless to humans and animals when they've dried on the plant, and leave no residues in the soil. These are the only two that we ever use, and they work extremely well.

They're non-selective – that is, they'll kill garden plants too – but they're tremendously useful in a number of situations. As sprays, they can be used on whole neglected areas and once the weeds have died back you can plant immediately. Where deep rooted weeds are growing close to garden plants, paint the leaves with

Tumbleweed gel, taking care not to get any on the surrounding vegetation. Most weeds succumb to the first dose, but the really vigorous types may need several applications.

Loose mulches: Mulching with compost, well rotted manure or bark chippings keeps down annual weeds and smothers out perennials – a 7.5cm/3in layer should do the trick.

Sheet mulches: Impervious mulches such as black plastic or old carpet are invaluable for clearing large areas. Most perennial weeds will be completely smothered out in one growing season, though more persistent types may need two. Black plastic can also be used in weed-infested borders, disguised with a thin layer of soil or one of the loose mulches. A thick layer of newspaper can be used in the same way, and will eventually rot down into the soil. Alternatively, lay down a porous membrane like Plantex when planting borders – it allows rain through but entirely suppresses weeds.

Plants: Set a thief to catch a thief – garden plants are the best and most decorative weed control of all, so plant as densely as you dare, using a good proportion of ground cover plants. Once they're growing well, weeds are deprived of light and will give up the unequal struggle.

Stinging nettles

Top Ten Weeds

Groundsel

❀ **BINDWEED (Convolvulus)**
This perennial climber has white trumpet flowers and thick ropes of smooth, off-white root which quickly colonise new areas, sending up further stems. Digging out the roots helps, but any overlooked portion will resprout. In large, uncultivated areas, spray with weedkiller or smother with black plastic. Where it is growing through garden plants, persistently pull the emerging stems or keep applying Tumbleweed gel.

❀ **BRAMBLES**
Though the blackberries may be tempting, brambles send out rooting runners and grow into substantial thickets if not controlled. Established plants are virtually impossible to dig out, so try starving them. Cut down the existing stems to ground level (wearing stout gloves), then do the same to any ensuing growth. The effort of continually producing new shoots will exhaust the plant within a year. If you prefer to use weedkiller,

you will probably have to make several applications.

❀ **CHICKWEED**
Chickweed forms a sprawling, low-growing mass of small leaves and tiny white flowers. This is a very persistent annual, and should be hoed or hand-pulled as soon as you spot it.

❀ **COUCH GRASS**
Also known as 'twitch' or 'scutch' grass. The creeping white roots send up stems of broad-leaved grass at regular intervals. Any small portion of root can resprout and the same methods as for bindweed should be used to eradicate it .

❀ **DANDELION**
There are several varieties of this perennial, but all have the familiar yellow sun-ray flowers and rosettes of toothed leaves, and the deep tap root is a real menace. Where it's impossible to dig it out (in paving or close to plants, for instance), apply a weedkiller such as Tumbleweed gel to young leaves. In lawns, spot-weed with Elliott Touchweeder.

❀ **DOCK**
A perennial with long lance-shaped leaves and tall plumes of rusty seedheads, sometimes as much as 90cm/3ft high. The deep tap roots are very tenacious but can be eliminated in the same way as dandelions.

❀ **GROUND ELDER**
This low-growing perennial has leaves and flowers which closely resemble those of the elder tree. Creeping underground stems throw up an

advancing army of shoots. Digging has some effect (though it will resprout from any pieces you miss), as will a mulch at least 10cm/4in deep. Alternatively, treat the emerging spring leaves with weedkiller and repeat the operation in summer.

❀ **GROUNDSEL**
Groundsel is an annual which grows to around 30cm/1ft with small yellow thistle-shaped flowers. Hoe or hand-weed, but if the plant is in

Dandelions

IDEAS FOR LOW MAINTENANCE

✔ *Careful grouting between paving slabs will save you endless hours of fiddly weeding.*

✔ *Don't worry too much about lawn weeds. Daisies are pretty and clover is beneficial (it adds nitrogen). Anything more thuggish can very quickly be spot-weeded with Elliott Touchweeder which kills lawn weeds but not the grass.*

✔ *Weeds that creep in from a neighbouring garden can be a real menace. Some are so deep-rooted that there's little you can do, but for ground elder, creeping buttercups and nettles, a physical barrier (of thick polythene for instance) set in the ground to a depth of 45cm/18in will keep them out.*

WEEDING TIPS

✔ *Don't forget that annual weeds can germinate and set seed in mild spells in winter, so keep the hoe handy.*

✔ *If you can't beat them, eat them. Ground elder can be cooked like spinach, nettles made into soup and dandelion, bittercress and chickweed leaves added to salads.*

✔ *Follow weedkiller instructions to the letter.*

UNDERSTANDING THE ENEMY

Weeds fall into two broad categories – annual nuisances and perennial pests.

Annual weeds are shallow rooted and rely on the quick production of masses of seed to keep the family going, and some can raise several generations in a year. Fortunately, most are easy to hoe or hand-weed.

Perennial weeds are a more diverse group, with several nasty tricks up their sleeves. Some form a deep taproot which clings tenaciously and if the top of the root is snapped off, the remainder will usually resprout.

Other perennials, such as brambles, increase from running stems which root where they touch the ground, and a variation on this theme is those like ground elder which send up stems from creeping roots.

flower, always break the stem – an intact plant has enough remaining energy to set seed even after you've put it on the compost heap.

❁ HAIRY BITTERCRESS

This tiny annual has many-lobed cress-like leaves arranged in a rosette, spikes of tiny white flowers and long narrow seedpods which explode when ripe. It's easy enough to hand-pull or hoe, but try to catch it before the seeds are set.

❁ NETTLES

Hairy leaved stinging nettles are one of the easier perennials to get rid of (so long as you wear gloves). The fibrous yellow roots creep and throw up new stems, but they're shallow enough to dig up in their entirety. In awkward places where you can't dig, spray the patch with Round-up or Tumbleweed.

THE MOST FEARSOME WEEDS OF ALL

Horsetail

The most appalling thugs in the world of weeds are **Japanese knotweed** and **horsetail** (sometimes called mare's tail), though fortunately they're localised rather than widespread. Japanese knotweed forms great stands of pinkish bamboo-like stems and broad oval leaves, with loose sprays of white flowers, to a height of 2.4m/8ft or more. Horsetail is a prehistoric plant which emerges rather like an erect, dull green bottle-brush.

They're so vigorous that you need a good deal of persistence to get rid of them. The roots go so deep that digging is no use at all, and pulling the tops off is a life sentence. If the invasion's not yet too serious, chemicals should work – crush the leaves and stems when plants are growing strongly in summer and apply a weedkiller containing glyphosate, such as Round-up or Tumbleweed. Several applications will probably be needed. For more serious infestations, it's best to smother them out. Laying black polythene over the whole area will deprive them of light and eventually kill them off, though it may take up to two years to eliminate them completely.

Japanese knotweed

Index

bedding plants 9–15
  aftercare 10, 13, 93, 94
  buying 9–10
  in containers 14–15, 33
  overwintering 11, 12, 14
  planting 9, 10, 14, 15
  top ten 14–15
bulbs 17–21
  aftercare 19, 20, 21, 92, 93
  in containers 29, 33
  indoor 18, 20
  naturalising 20, 21
  overwintering 21
  planting 17, 19

climbers and wall shrubs 23–7
  see also plain roses
  aftercare 25, 92
  in containers 29, 34
  low-maintenance 87
  over fruit trees 37
  planting 23
  pruning 24, 26–7
  supporting 23, 25, 34, 98
  top ten 26–7
colour harmony 13, 19, 47, 53, 55, 63, 99
compost making 113, 115
container gardening 14–15, 20–1, 29–35
  see also plain houseplants
  aftercare 30–1, 35
  composts 19, 29, 35, 105, 107, 125
  fruit 34, 38, 40, 41
  indoor 18
  pests/diseases 72, 91, 93–4
  planting 10, 19, 30, 35
  two-tier planting 17
  vegetables 35, 55, 125, 127, 128, 129
  water feature 132, 133, 135

fragrant plants
  bedding plants 13, 15, 59
  bulbs 18, 20–1
  climbers 26, 27
  hardy perennials 63, 65
  herbs 34, 67
  roses 100, 101, 102, 103
  shrubs 45, 107, 108, 109
  water plants 133, 134
fruit 37–41
  in containers 32, 34, 38, 40, 41
  pests and diseases 39, 40, 41, 92, 94, 95
  planting/aftercare 37
  pruning/training 37, 38, 39, 40, 41
  rose/clematis over tree 37

garden planning/design 43–7
  evergreen framework 43, 45, 69, 106
  low-maintenance 83–7
  making drawings 46
  re-designing 47
  screening eyesores 46
ground cover 47, 83–5, 87
  bulbs 21
  hardy perennials 65
  herbs 69
  roses 102, 103
  shrubs 27, 108
  strawberries 41

hanging baskets and window boxes 14–15, 53–9
  planting/aftercare 54, 93
  security 56
  top ten plants 57–9
hardy perennials 61–5
  foliage plants 62
  low-maintenance 87
  planting/aftercare 61, 64, 65, 92, 95
  top ten 64–5
hedging 43, 45, 69, 106
herbs 67–9
  in containers 29, 34, 55, 67, 68, 69
  hedging/edging 69, 106, 126
  top ten 68–9
houseplants 71–5
  see also plain container gardening
  aftercare 71–2, 74, 91, 93–4
  creating microclimate 75
  hazards 74, 75
  top ten 74–5
  troubleshooting 72, 75

lawns 77–81
  aftercare 79–81
  low-maintenance 83
  mowers 79, 81
  renovation 79
  seeding/turfing 77–9
  troubleshooting 81
  weeds 77, 78, 81, 138
low-maintenance garden 83–7
  ground cover 83–5
  top-choice plants 86–7
  watering 87

making the most of
  clematis 24, 25, 37
  fuchsias 12
  geraniums 11
  houseplants 73

peonies 63
raised vegetable beds 126
roses 37, 98, 100
water lilies 133
weed beaters 84–5
winter colour 56
moving plants 44
mulching 37, 87, 114–15
  pebble 27, 35
  sheet materials 84, 86, 129

pests and diseases 89–95
  bulbs 19, 20, 21
  clematis 24
  controls 89, 90, 91–5
  fruit 39, 40, 41
  hardy perennials 64, 65
  identification 91–5
  indoor 72
  lawns 81
  roses 97, 100
  seedlings 50
  vegetables 127, 128, 129
  water gardening 133
propagation 49–51
  cuttings 11, 12, 14, 50–1, 106, 109
  division 62, 65, 74
  from seed 49–50, 94
  layering 109
  plantlets/offsets 74
  runners 41

roses 97–103
  climbing on fruit trees 37
  companion planting 99
  containers 34, 99, 102, 103
  disease-resistant 103
  low-maintenance 87
  planting/aftercare 34, 97–8
  pruning 98, 100
  rose sickness 97
  top choices 101–3
  troubleshooting 100

shady sites 45
  bedding/bulbs 14, 15, 20
  climbers/wall shrubs 25, 26, 87
  containers 30, 35, 57, 58
  fruit 37, 41
  ground cover 84–5
  hardy perennials 62, 64–5
  herbs 67
  indoor 71, 74, 75
  roses 102
  shrubs 105, 107, 108, 109
  trees 121, 123
  water gardening 131, 135
shrubs 105–9
  see also plain climbers and wall shrubs

in containers 29, 31, 34–5, 105, 107
  hedging 43, 45, 106
  lime haters/acid lovers 105, 107, 111, 115
  low-maintenance 86
  pests and diseases 92, 94
  planting/aftercare 105
  pruning 31, 106, 108, 109
  top ten 108–9
soil 111–15
  conditioners 114–15
  improvement 67, 77, 111–12, 117, 126
  types 107, 108, 111–12
support systems
  climbers 23, 25, 34, 99, 102
  peony 63
  soft fruit 39, 41

topiary, forming box ball 31
trees 117–23
  aftercare 92, 94, 119
  container gardening 29, 35
  formative pruning 119
  low-maintenance 86
  planting/staking 117, 118
  small garden 119
  top choices 121–3

vegetables 125–9
  in containers 35, 55, 125, 127, 128, 129
  in flower borders 126
  from seed 49
  raised beds 126
  top choices 127–9
  troubleshooting 93, 94, 127, 128, 129

water gardening 131–5
  bubble pool 132
  child safety 132
  planting/aftercare 132, 135
  pool construction 131–2
  top ten plants 134–5
  troubleshooting 133
  tubs/barrels 132, 133, 135
weed control 137–9
  mulching 84, 137, 138, 139
  safety precautions 139
  top ten weeds 138–9
  weedkillers 84, 137, 138, 139
window boxes
  see also hanging baskets and window boxes
winter colour 15, 56, 58, 65
  bulbs 17
  shrubs 26, 35, 45, 59, 86, 108, 109
  trees 45, 86, 120, 121–2

Garden Notes

£5

worth

of

vouchers

Redemption value 0.001p

£1.00 OFF COUPON

TO THE CUSTOMER
This coupon can be used in part payment against a 75L sack of Levington Multi-Purpose Compost. Do not embarass your retailer by asking him to redeem against another item. He is not empowered to do so. Valid in the UK and Eire only until 31st August 1997. Not exchangeable for cash.

TO THE RETAILER
Levington Horticulture Ltd will redeem this coupon at its face value provided ONLY that it has been taken in part payment for a 75L sack of Levington Multi-Purpose Compost. Levington Horticulture Ltd reserves the right to refuse payment against misredeemed coupons. Please submit coupons to Levington Horticulture Ltd, Garden Advisor, Paper Mill Lane, Bramford, Ipswich, Suffolk IP8 4BZ. Closing date for submission: 30th November 1997.

Valid until 31st August 1997

Redemption value 0.001p

£1.00 OFF COUPON

TO THE CUSTOMER
This coupon can be used in part payment against a 1L bottle of Tomorite. Do not embarass your retailer by asking him to redeem against another item. He is not empowered to do so. Valid in the UK and Eire only until 31st August 1997. Not exchangeable for cash.

TO THE RETAILER
Levington Horticulture Ltd will redeem this coupon at its face value provided ONLY that it has been taken in part payment for a 1L bottle of Tomorite. Levington Horticulture Ltd reserves the right to refuse payment against misredeemed coupons. Please submit coupons to Levington Horticulture Ltd, Garden Advisor, Paper Mill Lane, Bramford, Ipswich, Suffolk IP8 4BZ. Closing date for submission: 30th November 1997.

Valid until 31st August 1997

Redemption value 0.001p

£1.50 OFF COUPON

TO THE CUSTOMER
This coupon can be used in part payment against a 250ml concentrate size of Murphy Tumbleweed. Do not embarass your retailer by asking him to redeem against another item. He is not empowered to do so. Valid in the UK and Eire only until 31st August 1997. Not exchangeable for cash.

TO THE RETAILER
Levington Horticulture Ltd will redeem this coupon at its face value provided ONLY that it has been taken in part payment for a 250ml concentrate size of Murphy Tumbleweed. Levington Horticulture Ltd reserves the right to refuse payment against misredeemed coupons. Please submit coupons to Levington Horticulture Ltd, Garden Advisor, Paper Mill Lane, Bramford, Ipswich, Suffolk IP8 4BZ. Closing date for submission: 30th November 1997.

Valid until 31st August 1997

Redemption value 0.001p

£1.50 OFF COUPON

TO THE CUSTOMER
This coupon can be used in part payment against a 70m² container of Murphy Ultra.. Do not embarass your retailer by asking him to redeem against another item. He is not empowered to do so. Valid in the UK and Eire only until 31st August 1997. Not exchangeable for cash.

TO THE RETAILER
Levington Horticulture Ltd will redeem this coupon at its face value provided ONLY that it has been taken in part payment for a 70m² container of Murphy Ultra. Levington Horticulture Ltd reserves the right to refuse payment against misredeemed coupons. Please submit coupons to Levington Horticulture Ltd, Garden Advisor, Paper Mill Lane, Bramford, Ipswich, Suffolk IP8 4BZ. Closing date for submission: 30th November 1997.

Valid until 31st August 1997

GARDEN NOTES